Yachts in a Hurry

SAGA

The striking commuter produced by Wheeler Shipyards of New York City, for Charles S. Payson. She is shown running at speed, shortly after her launching in 1935. Powered then by twin V-12 Packards but changed later to twin V-12 Wright Typhoons with the addition of an enclosed bridge. The author's pride and joy in the 1960s. She was fast and wet.

Yachts in a Hurry

An Illustrated History of the Great Commuter Yachts

C. Philip Moore

Foreword by Robert B. MacKay

W. W. Norton & Company

New York   London

The text of the book is composed in Fairfield Medium
with the display set in Fournier
Composition and book design by The Sarabande Press
Manufacturing by The Courier Corporation

ISBN 0-393-03576-X

W.W. Norton & Company, Inc., 500 Fifth Avenue, New York, N.Y. 10110
W.W. Norton & Company, Ltd., 10 Coptic Street, London WC1A 1PU

1 2 3 4 5 6 7 8 9 0

Contents

The New York Yacht Club Station at 26th Street

Foreword

—————

IN 1900, THE BROOKLYN DAILY EAGLE REPORTED THAT LONG ISLAND'S "North Shore, in fact . . . the entire eastern portion of the Island, is within easy, comfortable commuting distance of Wall Street." The article went on to explain, "Suppose you are 5 to 10 miles from the shore, it merely means 25 minutes or so in your carriage, you jump on your yacht, and there you are." Two years later, the New York *Herald* informed its readers that "an enormous fleet of private yachts carry owners at racing speed twice a day from their great estates to the wharf on Manhattan Island nearest their offices."

Commuting by water had become a seasonal phenomenon and soon gave birth to a whole new class of vessels that were to become known as "commuters" or "business boats." By the 1920s, these boats had been given a boost by the introduction of the high-powered combustion engine developed during World War I for aircraft. Powered by these new engines, commuters could achieve speeds of 30 to 50 knots as they whisked their citybound owners from estates to Wall Street in just an hour.

The phenomenon was not so much sparked by discovery on the part of country gentry of a new method of reaching the city, but the reverse. It was the desire of Manhattan's affluent to build houses in resort areas so they could experience country life in season and participate in new forms of recreation taking place there ranging from golf to polo that led to commuting by water. So popular did this mode of transportation become that, between 1860 and 1940, when more than 950 country houses were built on Long Island, virtually every major estate built along the shore can be linked to a commuter. Indeed, many thought that ownership of a commuter was a prerequisite of country life. The recently discovered building records for Wilton Lloyd-Smith's 1928 Lloyd Neck estate, for example, are interspersed with invoices for *Argo*, a 60-foot commuter yacht, which was being constructed at the same time. Nor were those who chose to commute by water necessarily yachtsmen. Many of its great adherents, such as financier Otto Kahn, never evidenced an interest in the pastime.

Helping to popularize the use of commuters was press coverage, not only in the yachting magazines, which featured photos of the latest commuters being built by the great yards in every issue, but also in the dailies—the *New York Times*, for example, reported at length on the construction of such yachting thoroughbreds as Harrison Williams's *Whim III* in 1928. Of course, *Country Life in America,* the periodical designed for country house owners (and those who would have liked to own estates in the country), played its part, which was not surprising since its publisher, Nelson Doubleday, was a commuter owner. Nor were these connections lost on the builders and engine manufacturers whose ads were run in both yachting and non-yachting periodicals. The Consolidated Shipbuilding Corporation reminded readers that commuters were "as necessary to Long Island as the motor car," and the Sterling Engine Company went so far as to picture a commuter in one of its color ads from the the thirties in front of a well-known Long Island country club, on whose lawns could be seen fashionable figures with the implements of half a dozen different sports. A subtle reminder to the titans of finance and industry of how to make the most of their affluence.

Country Life in America even offered its readers a photo-essay on the new form of commuting in which Mr. John W. Kaiser of Glen Cove, Long Island, was shown being rowed out to his commuter, where he settled into a large wicker chair on the fantail to scan the *Wall Street Journal* before being served breakfast by the steward. He later joined his captain on the bridge to catch a glimpse of Gotham's skyline before stepping ashore at Wall Street. The actual commuting experience could, in fact, be even more posh. Typically, owners were picked up at their docks or from their yacht clubs, often clad only in their nightgowns since they waited to don their business attire on board. It appears, however, that there were many variations in routine. Jeremiah Milbank's son recalls that his father was in the habit of coming out to Greenwich, Connecticut, for dinner and then returning on *Jem* (later *Jessica*) to Manhattan at night so he could be there first thing in the morning. The sons of James D. Mooney, a vice-chairman of General Motors, remember that their father would walk to the end of his Centre Island dock in Oyster Bay promptly at 7:30 A.M. clad only in his bathing suit. Captain H.R.O. Johnson, a highly decorated World War I veteran, would already have the twin Liberties purring aboard *Rosemarie* (her previous owner, the composer Rudolf Friml, had named the swift 50-footer for his famous operetta) and Mr. Mooney's mail and the daily papers already on board. Halfway down the Sound toward Manhattan, Captain Johnson would cut off the engines and Mr. Mooney would take an invigorating morning dip before dressing for work. George F. Baker could summon *Little Viking* to the dock of his summer home, Viking's Cove, near Matinecock Point by pushing a button on an instrument panel in his bedroom. This activated a special signaling device on the roof, which could not only summon his commuter, but also the launches from his 272-foot yacht, *Viking*, or his 72-foot racing sloop, *Ventura*. Fond of showing motion pictures to his weekend guests on calm summer evenings, Baker would direct that the mainsail be raised aboard *Ventura* so that movies could be projected onto it from the bridge of the nearby *Viking*. Roused by such a screening late one night, the over-served wife of one of his neighbors staggered out on her balcony

9

and thereafter proclaimed that she had seen cowboys and Indians riding down Long Island Sound.

Commuters could also be used to entertain. They provided agile platforms from which to view America's Cup and Harvard–Yale boat races, for example, and they could also be used to access events ashore. Franklin "Doggie" Ellis, who worked on several commuters in the thirties, including one belonging to Governor Lowell Weicker's grandfather, could remember many evenings spent waiting for its owner's party to return from the theater before heading home. It is even recorded that for the Annual Dinner of the Seawanhaka Corinthian Yacht Club on September 15, 1910, E. P. Whitney's *Arrow* and Peter Rouse's *Winchester* shuttled the club's entire membership out to their Centre Island station and then back to the city.

Commuting by water was also in vogue from Long Island's South Shore, Connecticut, the Hudson River, and the Jersey Shore; so much so, in fact, that during rush hours, the East River was jammed with boats having to raft three-to-four-deep at docks such as those maintained by the River Club and the New York Yacht Club, while others lay at anchor as far as the eye could see or tied up to piers on the Brooklyn and Jersey waterfronts. Nor was New York City the nation's only water-commuting destination; Boston, Detroit, and Philadelphia were among the other cities where it was tried.

Of course, no method of commuting is without its problems. Charles S. Payson, who later built *Saga*, one of the greatest commuters, first commuted on a yacht tender that had proved too heavy for davit use until he hit a submerged mattress in the East River at speed. Mrs. Henry Sears recalls that she was always prepared to dine alone on days when her husband commuted by water, since fouled propellers and other breakdowns were frequent. In fact, "Doggie" Ellis remembered going through twenty-seven wheels (propellers) in a single season due to debris in the river. Commuting could even be dangerous; explosions were not uncommon before the advent of efficient blowers, and then there was always the unexpected.

Drayton Cochran recalled one such trip while singlehandedly running a small commuter home down a calm Long Island Sound one

Spring afternoon. Feeling the need to relieve himself, he left the wheel and stepped to the transom in time-honored sailor fashion, failing to notice the wake that was headed his way. Thrown overboard, Cochran swam several miles to a government mark, where he spent an uncomfortable night banging a gong clapper for help. His boat was discovered run up on the Connecticut shore near his home in Darien by a policeman making his rounds on a bicycle. Unaware that the fuel lines had sheared on impact, he made the terrible mistake of lighting a match in the cabin!

Freeloading was also a frequent problem. The late Jack Stafford, captain of Marshall Field's Gar Wood–built commuter, *Corisande*, recalled in the January 1988 issue of *Power and Motor Yacht* that: "Half the people of Cold Spring Harbor would get on the boat to ride in. It got so there were a lot of people you didn't know. Mr. Field would say to me, 'Who's that? Friend of yours?' I'd say, 'No, I thought he was yours!' "

The Great Depression, Robert Moses's new parkways, and the use of seaplanes for commuting, which lured away such devotees as Marshall Field, were among the long litany of changes that curtailed commuting by water during the thirties. It was in 1938, in fact, that the New York Yacht Club gave up its East River landing, although "Doggie" Ellis, referring to the tax policies of the New Deal, dismissed all but one cause . . . "Roosevelt."

Now the passage of time has made the phenomenon of commuting by water seem as remote as the life and times of George Washington. Only a few are left who can even recall the practice, but just as this interesting chapter in the history of yachting was about to pass into obscurity, Phil Moore, a former owner of *Saga*, has come forward with this wonderful account of these yachting thoroughbreds, their power plants, owners and builders. It has not been an easy job—the phenomenon went largely unrecorded and much of the information that has appeared in print is contradictory. There are virtually no pictures of commuters in use in this period other than glimpses of them in spectator fleets viewing cup races. Apparently, those who found commuters the best way to get to work never thought to record it—it was the daily routine and too mundane to be worth photographing. Phil Moore, however, has been relentless in his search for every shred of information about these yachts and has produced between these covers a comprehensive study beautifully illustrated with images from Mystic Seaport's Rosenfeld Collection (which in most instances, depict these yachts in pristine state during their sea trials).

Phil has also been at the forefront of the revival of interest in the surviving commuter yachts, helping to make possible the 1989 and 1991 Commuter Rendezvous, chronicled in Chapter 5. The 1991 event even featured a commuting run into New York from Long Island and Connecticut ports such as Oyster Bay and Greenwich with a number of CEOs on board. Participants were able to get some sense of what it must have been like to commute during the era of these great flyers as commuters raced down the East River, often three and four abreast flashing by Manhattan's skyscrapers. Captain Raymond Thoms, then in his fifth decade as skipper of *Jessica,* having served every owner of that handsome vessel, was even heard to remark as he surveyed the scene from his bridge, "Just like old times!"

ROBERT B. MACKAY, PH. D., is Director of the Society for the Preservation of Long Island Antiquities and co-owner of *Red Witch,* a 38 foot commuter.

Preface

M OST OF THIS BOOK COVERS THE GOLDEN AGE OF COMMUTERS, THE years between the two world wars when commuting by water was both novelty and convenience for the wealthy, sporting business leaders of the 1920s and 1930s. The entire period covered is approximately a hundred years, beginning in 1869 with the steam yachts of the late nineteenth century. Most of the boats in this book are true yachts in a hurry—commuters able to sustain a speed of at least 18 miles per hour—15 knots—and they are, as the photos in this book make clear, very rakish machines indeed.

In researching, writing about, and listing these sundry craft, events, and personalities of the past, some unavoidable and troublesome confusion came with the territory. I assumed that the knowledgeable people I interviewed were honest and experienced. But I know they were also human—which is to say, not infallible. Their facts—and mine—are also subject to the eroding influence of time. So there may be errors in this book.

Prior to the 1930s, no restrictions were placed on the naming of yachts. The data, dimensions, specifications, and ownership are as accurate as can be found at the present time. When there were differences or discrepancies I referred in depth to the venerable, but also not infallible, Lloyd's Register of American Yachts.

Although there were other efforts to list American yachts—the first in 1872, Fox's Yacht Annual, lasted only a few years—Lloyd's endured the longest: from 1903 until 1976. In 1760 a group of marine underwriters, who gathered regularly in Edward Lloyd's coffeehouse in London, formed a committee for the purpose of issuing a register giving the details of ships likely to be offered to them for insurance. The first existing register of merchant ships is dated 1764, and included in the details was an assessment of each ship's condition, the vowels A,E,I,O,U indicating the state of the hull in descending order of merit, and the letters G,M,B (good, middling, bad) the state of the equipment. In order to make an assessment the craft had to be examined, and to this end the underwriters employed a handful of men with a knowledge of shipping, retired ship captains and the like who were the forerunners of the highly trained surveyors of today. In 1834, after competition with another registry, the society assumed its present form, with the title of Lloyd's Register of British and Foreign Shipping.

Since 1775 the highest classification was indicated by the now famous symbol A1, and the desire of shipowners to have their craft placed in the top grade led to requests from shipbuilders for guidance as to the standard required. The result was the issue by the society of rules for the construction and maintenance of these craft.

At the request of leading British yachtsmen, the society extended its scope to include pleasure craft, special rules being drawn up for the construction of yachts. The rules were published in the yacht register, first issued in that year. The first Lloyd's Register of American Yachts was published in May 1903. According to the society, "an entry in the Register of American Yachts does not constitute either classification or official registration. Classification is referred to later in the Key, whilst registration, not being a function of Lloyd's Register of Shipping, is dealt with by the National Authority of the Country to which the yacht belongs. In the United States it is effected through the Bureau of Customs, represented by the Collector of Customs at the Port of Registry chosen by the owner." Originally it was not the practice to include motor yachts of under 35 feet in length on the water line. In the 1970s, the last years of Lloyd's Register, a publication fee of ten dollars for each yacht listed was charged.

The A1 symbol and the Lloyd's Register of Shipping have been synonymous for over 230 years—a long and prestigious history. To fully understand the body of information available in Lloyd's Register, the Explanation of Contents at the beginning of each volume should be read in its entirety. The colorful Private Signals of Yachtsmen section of Lloyd's shows some striking originality in amateur flag designing. Even though Lloyd's is the yachtman's bible it is subject to errors, as I found out in my listing of Saga (Nipper) in the 1962 edition. "Designer: John Whacker" should have been "Designer: John Wheeler," although a combination of Hacker and Wheeler could have been only for the good.

In compiling this book it has not been possible to include every significant vessel. Undoubtedly, someone's favorite yacht has been left out. Confusion may result in cases of two or more commuters having the same name, or the same vessel having more than one name in the past. Some, owned by the famous, are easy to track; others of lesser note, but still significant, lie in dusty oblivion. As I have said, the history and specifications of many boats are inconsistent in the sources. If I have erred, please forgive me. I had accuracy in mind.

C.P.M.

Look on my works, ye mighty, and despair.
PERCY BYSSHE SHELLEY

Acknowledgments

I BEGAN COMPILING DATA, INFORMATION, AND LISTINGS ON COM-
muters about thirty-five years ago when I was the involved owner
(or was it the other way around) of the lovely *Saga*. To say that this
book on commuters would not have been possible without the help
of the following people is not strictly true—it simply would have
taken more years and then would have been inferior in many ways.
The following special people gave me much inspiration, knowledge,
and cooperation.

With deepest thanks and gratitude, I dedicate this book to these
wonderful individuals:

Nancy—my wife and best friend
Joe Gribbons—a mine of nautical knowledge.
Mike and Ann Matheson—true Commuter aficionados.
Jim and Tony Lewis—foremost antique boating enthusiasts.

And last but not least, I am everlastingly indebted to Jim Mairs,
W.W. Norton's intrepid editor, who although a rag sailor, encouraged

ACKNOWLEDGMENTS me to produce this book and whose patience and help have brought it to existence.

Others to whom I am indebted are as follows: Danny Aciero; Dick Ambler; Gerry and Paula Conover; Henry Austin Clark; Ed and Maggie Cutts; Jennifer Elliott; Tom Fexas; Peter Freebody; Giffy Full; Ben Fuller; Mrs. Gordon Hamersley; Halsey Herreshoff; Jay Higgins; Tim Hodgon; Louie Howland III; John Kellogg; Timmy Larr; Bill Luders; Bob MacKay; Allan McInnis, Anson Moore; John and Margie Pannell; George U. Pattinson; Phred Philmore; Stanley Rosenfeld; Garry and Ingred Scherb; Phil Sharpless; Peter Spector; Capt. Ray Thombs; Ted Valpey Jr.; Doug Van Patton; Capt. Hermann Voss; Margery Warren; Jon Wilson; Wilson Wright; and Jim Wynne.

Yachts in a Hurry is being published in conjunction with the Mystic Seaport and its extensive Rosenfeld Photo Collection. I much appreciate their valued and ongoing help. I wish to thank J. Revel Carr; Debbie Digregorio; Dana Hewsen; Jack MacFarland; Jerry Morris; Elisabeth Parker Rafferty; Mary Ann Stets; Ellen Stone; and Peter Vermilua.

Yachts in a Hurry

Introduction

Extravagant Travelers

THE QUIET OF A SEPTEMBER MORNING ON MANHASSET BAY IS broken by the sudden deep roar of a large, aircraft-type marine engine, accompanied like cannon fire by a burst of smoke. The engine is coaxed into smoothness, and then its twin—another big 12-cylinder—adds to the crescendo and is tuned down until the two rumble in unison. Even though the residents of this elite little community have grown accustomed to this mechanical reveille that echoes from Port Washington to Great Neck, it is always an abrupt awakening.

Soon a maroon-and-black V-16 Cadillac phaeton glides up to the pier where the long, low, white-hulled beauty waits, reverberating with the promise of speed. An older gentleman in a gray suit alights with ease from the running board of the car and crosses the lawn to the dock. With a slight nod to the uniformed crew, he steps aboard and surveys the hazy harbor. The lines are cast off and the owner settles into the after cockpit, shaking out the New York *Herald Tribune*. A light breakfast on a silver tray is set before him. At a slight gesture the Captain comes aft, and they both confer. The long white hull moves out with a smooth increase of engine tempo.

Cruising slowly to the head of the bay and into the open water of Long Island Sound, the white boat is followed by another, this one sleek and black, her Wright Typhoon engines rumbling and the day's first sunlight flashing on her brightwork. As the two boats reach open water, their exhaust notes increase to an unharnessed roar. The race to Wall Street is on!

As the throttles are moved forward, the great hulls chatter through the light chop. Running easily, they climb on top of the waves and surge ahead at increasing speed, their wakes steady as they fan out aft. These are commuter yachts running at flank speed, dueling down the last of Long Island Sound, past Throgs Neck, sending their wakes splashing on North and South Brother Islands, maneuvering through Hell Gate, shooting down the crowded East River.

As they pass Blackwells Island, the East River Drive traffic slows to watch these express yachts in competition on the narrowing river. Under the three bridges they flash down to Wall Street where the contest is ended. Who is the winner on this hazy autumn morning? With relief the crews come on deck as the two boats ease into the docks. They secure the fenders and then the lines. Three other commuters are already tied up, their decks being washed down. This has been an exciting start to the day, and the gentlemen wave hello as they step off the still-rumbling boats. Down the pier they go to the tiny streets and tall financial towers of Lower Manhattan. The winner of this close race will not be decided until they run back to Long Island in the late afternoon.

Something like this was a typical morning drama during the Roaring Twenties, a time when fleets of commuter yachts docked in Manhattan and raced twice a day on the rivers, when gentlemen in other waterfront cities enjoyed the convenience of fast personal ferries to take them to and from work, when naval architects and boatbuilders specialized in varieties of these yachts in a hurry, when an advertisement in a yachting magazine proclaimed, "Down the bay, up the river, in from outside—you see these fleet, rakish, swagger-looking craft speeding hundreds of busy executives to downtown offices, refreshed and eager for a great day's work."

Commuters were an extravagance in every way. Most of them were built and finished to the highest yacht standards. They were big speedboats engineered and powered with torpedo-boat sophistication. They burned extraordinary quantities of fuel and cost shocking amounts to maintain. They were tended by crews whose only business was to run them at wild speeds for a few hours each day and spend the time in between cleaning, polishing, oiling, and tuning these wonderful conveyances devoted to the whims and working routines of the titans of finance and industry.

The years between the two world wars were the golden age of yacht commuting, a time of low taxes and the fulfilled dreams of wealthy men with fortunes to spend and names like Vanderbilt, Morgan, Stroh, Ford, and Kennedy. But the beginnings of these rush-hour express cruisers go back more than fifty years to 1869 and beautiful Lake Windermere in England, where H. W. Schneider, a titan of England's iron industry, had a steam yacht built to carry him from his palatial home on the lake to the railroad siding where his private car awaited. The 65-foot *Esperance* spent many years as Schneider's "commuter"—but more about her later.

The era of the steam yacht was just beginning in the United States in the 1870s. By 1875 there were thirteen steam yachts in the New York Yacht Club fleet, ranging from 57 to 114 feet in length, some of them no doubt in use as commuters. By 1882 there were twenty-three steam yachts in the NYYC fleet, including the first of J. Pierpont Morgan's *Corsairs*, used by the great financier as a commuter from his Hudson River estate. By 1885, it had become customary for a number of steam yacht owners, many of them financial leaders, to commute on their yachts from country homes along the North Jersey coast, the Hudson River, and Long Island Sound to Lower Manhattan—some every day except in winter, others to get out of town for the weekend. In May of 1886 the New York Yacht Club obtained from the City of New York exclusive use of a pier at 26th Street on the East River, and the right to "place and maintain" a landing stage at the foot of 23rd Street on the Hudson for the exclusive use of yachts. By 1900, the NYYC listed 189 steam yachts, and many wealthy owners kept both a large, oceangoing steam yacht and a fast commuter, or "flyer," as they were called. Detroit and Boston had their own commuter fleets, and the competitive spirit of business leaders in all three cities spurred the development of ever-faster and ever-more-elegant vehicles to bring a man to work.

Commuters were anywhere from 25 to 300 feet or more in length. Their accommodations were generally minimal but plush. Speed was the foremost consideration, and speeds were sometimes astonishing. Before 1900, a 100- to 160-foot yacht was not considered an unusually large conveyance, and steam was the preferred method of propulsion. Steam yachts were expensive, however, with their large boilers, bunkers full of coal, pumps and tubes and gauges, licensed engineers and large crews. Steam was propulsion for the very rich—quiet, mechanically unfussy, and labor-intensive. The not-quite-so-rich entered the game at the beginning of the century when gasoline engines began to power yachts and workboats of all kinds, getting better and bigger every year and eventually eclipsing steam as the power plant of choice in boats for commuting—which is to say in boats for speed and style.

Altogether, more than three hundred of these boats of speed and style were built by about seventy firms. The principal yards that built steam-propelled commuters were the famous Herreshoff Manufacturing Company of Bristol, Rhode Island; the Charles L. Seabury and Gas Engine and Power Company—the renowned "Consolidated"— of Morris Heights, New York City; Yarrow Ltd. of East London in England; and Bath Iron Works of Bath, Maine. Commuters with gasoline engines were built by Consolidated; Purdy Boat Works, variously in Indiana, Michigan, Florida, and on Long Island; George F. Lawley and Son of Boston; American Car and Foundry (acf) of Wilmington, Delaware, an early stock boatbuilder; Robinson Marine Construction Company of Benton Harbor, Michigan, which built limousine-style speedboats; Luders Marine Construction Company

ARROW

One of the earliest commuters, Arrow, was designed by Charles Dell Mosher and capable of over 40 mph in 1902. This photo taken by Charles Edwin Bolles shows her full 132-foot length. A large searchlight, a canvas deck overhead, and a belly-band, rub-rail all have been added to the hull. Commodore Flint's private signal is flying from the mast.

of Stamford, Connecticut; Henry B. Nevins and Company, the famous City Island boatyard in New York City; and Chris-Craft of Algonac, Michigan. By the middle of the 1920s, according to builders' advertisements, hundreds of busy executives were "turning from the dusty, traffic-choked roads to the refreshing mode of transportation—commuting by water." There was not a lot of truth in advertising in the 1920s, but this seems to have been true.

More than fifty of these glamorous boats have survived. Some have been consistently cared for and valued over the years, many have been brought back to glory by careful restoration, and others await attention. The 1980s brought a resurgence of interest in commuters as a type—as a special, elite vehicle in the spectrum of antique boats of all kinds, much as dual-cowl phaetons occupy a special place in the world of antique and classic automobiles. Special and elite are appropriate here, as the photos in these pages will show.

My own involvement with these boats goes back nearly a lifetime, and by sheer luck developed into a relationship with one of the great ones—and one of the last ones—Charles Payson's 1935 *Saga*. My father's interest in motorboats was lifelong, at first on Lake Michigan with a naphtha launch and then on Long Island Sound. It was somewhat complicated, however, by my mother's lack of interest. My mother fainted occasionally in water over her knees and often became seasick aboard, sometimes when the family boat was still in the slip.

The first magazines I remember at the house were *Boy's Life, Popular Mechanics, Rudder,* and *Yachting.* Sitting with an issue of *Yachting* one summer afternoon, I came across the striking *Saga* pictured in color running out of Newport as a tender during the America's Cup summer of 1937. The love of boats was never out of mind from boyhood through career and family years, and in 1954 I quit the advertising business, took the big step and purchased a small boatyard in South Florida that bore a grandiose name: Lake Worth Yacht Basin (before 1960, what we now know as a marina was a "yacht basin," perhaps a better name). It was there while trying to make ends meet—the primary activity in all Florida boatyards at the time—that I again

SAGA

Running down Long Island Sound in 1935, her beautiful tapered stern is evident in this picture. Except for decks and overheads the entire boat was mahogany brightwork. With abundant power from her twin V-12s and good handling, she was one of the finest commuter.

heard about *Saga.* A fellow yacht broker in Miami told me about this long, low 60-foot flyer that might be coming on the market.

The boat was tracked down at the Merrill-Stevens yard in Miami, and she was indeed the beloved *Saga,* now renamed *Nipper.* She, or he (Nipper is defined in Webster's as a small boy), was then owned by Arthur Vining Davis, founder of the Aluminum Company of America. Beyond Alcoa, A. V. Davis was an investor in Florida enterprises and a Bahamas land developer, as well as chairman of the board of banks and corporations. After trying to get to Davis through his attorneys, one of Davis's representatives called a few weeks later at the Lake Worth Yacht Basin and suggested that I get down to Miami for a firsthand inspection of *Nipper.* A week later I met with Captain Herman Voss aboard the boat and was given a two-hour inspection tour. She was all I expected and more. In perfect condition, she was attended by a captain and hand on twenty-four-hour notice, and lay in a covered slip (Mr. Davis's own buildings, half of the Merrill-Stevens complex). At 69 feet and powered by three GM 6-71 diesels, *Nipper* was somewhat intimidating. This was lessened a little by the contrast with Mr. Davis's *Elda,* lying alongside. This was the large *Elda* at 167 feet. At the time, Arthur Vining Davis also had two smaller *Eldas*— 50 feet and 65 feet.

There was one slip at the Lake Worth Yacht Basin that would take a vessel as big as *Nipper.* Could she be purchased at a reasonable enough price to make it worthwhile? Why not? And so I made a very low offer with a small deposit, subject to a trial run. It all seemed too good to be true, and the possibility of owning such a yacht was put out of mind until six weeks later when I received a call from a Miami law firm asking if I was the person (nut) who had made the offer on Mr. Davis's *Nipper.* Then Captain Voss was put on the phone.

The Captain suggested that I come to Miami again, go for a trial run, and if everything was to my satisfaction meet with Mr. Davis to finalize the transaction. In somewhat of a daze I said yes and set a date.

In retrospect I see what a major adventure the acquisition of *Nipper* was. The trial run took us into heavy swells in the Atlantic with small-craft warnings flying. I ran *Nipper* on Biscayne Bay, but Captain Voss insisted that we go outside to get the feel of the boat. Obviously she could take more than I could. After a wet run powering into the seas outside Government Cut, we waited about a mile offshore for the right wave to appear so that we could turn around and run with following seas to the troubled inlet. We made it finally, but I would not like to do it again. The Captain passed this off, saying that conditions in the North Atlantic during the war were much worse. Captain Voss had experienced the North Atlantic aboard a German submarine during World War II. "*Nipper* iss strong but vet," he said.

The ride to Mr. Davis's home in the gray limo was much more soothing. Inside the mansion we were surrounded by rich furnishings and unobtrusive servants. Mr. Davis, although a small man, was a commanding presence—very businesslike, a gentleman of the old school. At the end of a short discussion during which he quizzed me on what I planned to do with his boat, he wrote his full signature on the salmon-colored document. It was exactly one inch in length. The transaction was completed.

Later, on the maiden voyage, my wife, son, and I maneuvered the heavy 69 feet of mahogany and oak down the narrow and crowded Miami River, then cruised gloriously up the Intracoastal past Fort Lauderdale, the Hillsborough Inlet, Boca Raton, and finally into Lake Worth with no charts and in squally weather. It was a saga in itself, worthy of the boat's old name. We changed her name back to *Saga*—it had to be lettered in twice because of the canoe stern. We also removed the 3-foot extended keel—used to cut through the sandy channels in Mr. Davis's Arvida developments in the Bahamas. With her wonderful sleek lines and beautiful mahogany joinery, she opened up a new world of cruising and on-board living. Usually all the kids were aboard when we cruised, although we left two behind at Mystic Seaport one summer and didn't realize it until we were headed up the Sound.

Saga was our part-time home for six memorable years of cruising the Bahamas, the Chesapeake, Long Island Sound, out to Nantucket. Many lasting friendships were made aboard with interesting people, a few quite knowledgeable about commuters. I put most of this into the log, and these random notes were the beginning of later research into the history and lore of commuters and their era. The era was finished by then, and so were many of the great commuters. While cruising in the summer of 1961, we took *Saga* to Essex and found the forlorn remains of *Aphrodite II* in the mud of a backwater off the Connecticut River.

In the late 1960s, with the kids growing older—sometimes not acting it—*Saga* was traded for an old Florida hotel. Almost since then we have tried to find her, to get her back. Ten years ago we were told that someone had seen her on the St. Johns River in Jacksonville where she was just a hull being towed to a breaker's yard.

So we and the world lost *Saga*—or so we think. I keep expecting to see her or hear of her one of these days as my interest in these boats takes me to antique-boat shows, old boatyards, and the restoration shops where commuters are being given new life in the 1990s. Failing that, we and the world have this book, where *Saga* appears running at speed on pages 2 and 27.

Chapter One

Steam Flyers

T HE FIRST MODERN COMMUTERS WERE STEAM YACHTS; BUT BEFORE
steam vessels became accepted as commuters, they had to be
accepted as yachts—or at least vessels fit for gentlemen. Although
steam was making nautical history in the early decades of the nineteenth century, and by 1838 two great steamships had crossed the
Atlantic with no assist from their sails, "steam" and "yacht" were still
thought an unsuitable combination. The early yacht clubs—the
Royal Yacht Squadron formed at East Cowes, England, in 1815, and
the New York Yacht Club, founded in 1844—were both sailormen's
clubs reluctant to accept the noisy, noisome, newfangled technology
of steam. In 1827 it was decreed by the Royal Yacht Squadron that
"any member applying a steam engine to his yacht shall be disquali-
fied thereby and cease to be a member." In 1843 the Squadron relent-
ed somewhat and permitted steam vessels in its fleet if they were over
100 tons, a concession made necessary when the Queen herself commissioned the steam yacht *Victoria and Albert* that year.

As mentioned in Chapter One, the first steam yacht to be built as a commuter, and now the oldest boat listed in *Lloyd's* Yacht Register, is *Esperance,* also considered to be the world's first twin-screw steam yacht. She was built in 1869 on the River Clyde by T. B. Seath and Company of Scotland for the great English industrialist H. W. Schneider. *Esperance* was transported with much difficulty by horse-cart from her Scottish building site down to Lake Windermere, the lovely lake in northwest England. Her hull is of the highest grade of iron, made by one of Schneider's companies, and the riveting is countersunk for an entirely smooth finish on the outside of the hull. According to the genial and knowledgeable owner of the Windermere Steamboat Museum, George H. Pattinson, the morning routine of *Esperance*'s owner was much like that of Wall Street commuters fifty and more years later. Schneider would leave his lakeside estate, Belsfield, preceded by a butler carrying his breakfast on a silver tray, and walk through gardens down to the *Esperance* pier. Breakfast was served in the paneled saloon of this 65′ × 10′ vessel during the journey to Lakeside where the industrialist boarded his own train to his factories and forges. By 1900 *Esperance* was owned by the Ferry Hotel on Lake Windermere, and remained in service until 1941 when she sank in 200 feet of water. That would have been the end of her had not the father of George H. Pattinson, who started collecting old steamboats before World War II, been determined enough to salvage her.

In the summer of 1988, while on the Antique and Classic Boat Society's tour of England, we were aboard *Esperance,* still proudly afloat in George Pattinson's Windermere Steamboat Museum. Sadly, her unique steam engine, in the form of an inverted V–twin to accommodate her two propellers, had been scrapped before the war. Her twin shafts and propellers were a novelty in the 1870s, and one boatman is said to have commented, when told of this unusual feature, "I suppose she must have a propeller at each end?" George Pattinson, who has already restored the ancient steam launch *Dolly,* at 140-plus years the oldest surviving mechanically propelled vessel in the world, sees no insurmountable problem in re-creating the original V-twin engine that pushed the first steam commuter more than 120 years ago.

While H. W. Schneider was on his way to work aboard *Esperance* in the 1870s, powerful men in New York were acquiring country homes and beginning to own the yachts that would become the kind of hearth-to-office transportation we now call commuters. In 1870 there were only four "power" yachts owned by members of the New York Yacht Club—and from 1870 to about 1900 power meant steam. In 1875 there were thirteen steam yachts listed in the NYYC fleet, ranging from 75 to 114 feet, although how many of these steamers were in use as commuters prior to 1880 is anybody's guess. There were twenty-three steam yachts in the NYYC fleet in 1882, including for the first time one called *Corsair,* the 185-foot steamer owned by J. Pierpont Morgan and used by the great financial wizard as a commuter between Cragston, his Hudson River country home, and his Manhattan offices. Before *Corsair,* J. P. Morgan had owned a launch called *Louisa* that took him across the Hudson from Cragston to the Garrison station of Commodore Vanderbilt's Hudson River Division, where he boarded a train for New York. *Louisa,* in service from 1873 to 1882, is almost certainly the first U.S. commuter.

Morgan's first *Corsair* was built by Cramp and Sons in Philadelphia in 1880. She was built for C. J. Osborn, another NYYC member, and Morgan bought her from Osborn in 1882. She was then the second-largest vessel in the club's fleet, and she was already named *Corsair.* (One of the Morgan myths is that this prince among robber barons named her *Corsair* in tribute to Henry Morgan, the Jamaican pirate of the 1600s, or for his own piratical proclivities—another myth, since Morgan was a brilliant organizer of money and resources, not a crass accumulator of wealth.) She was the beginning of a line of four magnificent *Corsairs* in the Morgan family.

J. Pierpont Morgan had bought his Hudson River estate in 1872 when he was thirty-five years old and still one of his father's faithful employees. He lived at Cragston for most of the rest of his life on weekends and at other times when his presence was not required in his austere offices downtown. Otherwise he lived on Madison Ave-

33

CORSAIR IV

Considered by many yachtsmen to be the most nearly perfect power yacht ever, Corsair IV was built for J.P. Morgan in 1930 by The Bath Iron Works, and used as a commuter. Steam turbo-electric power made her exceptionally smooth. She went down off Acapulco, Mexico, in 1949 while on a cruise.

nue in a house adjacent to the marble Morgan Library. By the middle of the 1880s, financial giants like Morgan began to use their yachts to commute from country homes on Long Island Sound or the Hudson to their city offices, and several yacht clubs maintained Manhattan docks and anchorages to accommodate them. A man admired and imitated, Morgan with his *Louisa* and later with his *Corsairs* must have influenced the phenomenon of yacht commuting.

In spite of the market failure in 1893—the "rich man's panic" in the middle of the otherwise opulent 1890s—more and more steam yachts were built for Gilded Age yachtsmen, although there was competition from other means of powering vessels—namely small gasoline engines being imported from Europe in the 1890s, Frank Ofeldt's amazing naphtha engines, and electric motors used primarily in smaller craft.

At the peak of the steam-yacht era, the wealthier and sportier power yachtsmen kept both a large oceangoing steam yacht and a fast commuter, or "flyer," in commission. These fast steamers, far more suitable for coping with the crowded waters of the Hudson and Hell Gate, were sometimes listed as launches, although they could be over 100 feet long and looked and went like torpedo boats. They were, in fact, civilian versions of the new, fast naval vessels being developed in America and Europe. Although most of the steam commuters flew the pennant of the New York Yacht Club, other clubs and cities were represented. The Albany, American, Beverly, Boston, Bristol, Detroit, Chicago, Hudson River and Knickerbocker yacht clubs, among others, had commuters in their fleets.

One of these clubs was totally devoted to power—i.e., steam— yachting, and it pioneered powerboat racing in America. The American Yacht Club was founded in Rye, NY, in 1883 by members of the NYYC for the use of and promotion of power boats only. The club announced its first race for steam yachts in 1891 with an unusually large cash prize of $500. Although a half-dozen of the "flyers" were invited, the event deteriorated until only William Randolph Hearst's *Vamoose* actually ran at 24 mph. In 1896 the American Yacht Club held its first race for naptha launches with three boats entered.

Between 1880 and 1900, interest in boats with engines—first reciprocating steam, then steam turbine, then naptha and electric, then gasoline—quickened and led to clubs, races, more sophisticated engines and hull forms and, of course, to commuters. By 1900 the remarkable Herreshoff Manufacturing Company of Bristol, Rhode Island, had designed and built close to 50 fast steam vessels for private and government use, and the firm's design and engineering wizard, Nathanael Greene Herreshoff, had designed more models and sizes of light steam engines than anyone else in the world.

In 1885 the Herreshoffs built a demonstration boat called *Stiletto*, arguably the prototype for all the steam flyers that came along in the next few decades. Her speed was almost unprecedented for the time. She made one eight-hour run at 23 knots or 26-1/2 miles an hour. The only faster modes of transportation in 1885 were the crack steam

Copyr'ld '92

VAMOOSE

This photograph of the early commuter was taken in 1892. Used for over thirty years, she was one of the swiftest of the early Nat Herreshoff designs. Powered by a 5-cylinder quadruple-expansion steam engine, she ran at 25 miles per hour.

trains. An athlete on a bicycle or aboard a fast horse could go over 20 miles an hour for a short distance, but only a steam yacht or an express train could cover distance in comfort and at sustained speed. And according to L. Francis Herreshoff the fast steam yacht was safer then than fast travel on shore. There was one more form of fast transportation, the great overnight and excursion steamboats, and *Stiletto* became famous for her run against the beautiful Hudson River steamboat *Mary Powell*, reputed to be the fastest power vessel in the United States.

Mary Powell was 300 feet long with clean lines, built for speed—reported to be as much as 25 knots—and as comfortable as a hotel. It was said that her captain, owner, and designer, Absalom Anderson, kept a boy aboard whose sole duty was to keep the flies from lighting on her rail and slowing her down by their weight. This legendary vessel's regular route was between Manhattan and mid-Hudson points, making a round trip each day. In fifty-eight years of service she never

36

had an accident and never lost a passenger. Until 1885 she never lost a race.

On June 10, 1885, Nat Herreshoff, designer of *Stiletto's* hull and all her machinery, ran his creation alongside the big sidewheeler for a few miles, then in a burst of speed swept ahead and crossed the bow of the fired-up *Mary Powell*, then slowed to let her pass, then opened up again and overhauled and shot past her. This was a convincing demonstration, and one that won enduring fame for the Herreshoff brothers. As a result, *Stiletto* was sold to the U.S. Navy in 1887 to be made into a torpedo boat. This was ten years after the Royal Navy's first seagoing torpedo boat, HMS *Lightning,* was built by John Thornycroft in Chiswick, England, and a dozen years after the first U.S. Navy torpedo boat, also called *Lightning,* was built by the Herreshoffs. *Stiletto* was used to deliver a spar torpedo—an explosive charge on a long pole—ancestor of the self-propelled torpedo developed in England in the 1870s.

In 1887 the Herreshoffs built a yacht similar to *Stiletto* for New York publisher Norman L. Munro, a flyer called *Now Then.* She was 85 feet long and made her delivery trip in 1887 from Newport to 24th Street, New York City, a distance of 170 miles, at the rate of 24 miles an hour. She became Norman Munro's commuter from his home on the North Jersey coast to Manhattan. The *Stiletto/Now Then* model was developed into other notable Herreshoff flyers such as *Scout, Lotus Seeker, Jean, Stroller, Clover, Vamoose,* and *Javelin.* It was a tribute to the Herreshoff Company's construction and engineering skills that two of these light but sturdy machines lasted for more than thirty years in demanding service. And elite service. The durable *Scout* was owned in turn by the Belmonts, Vanderbilts, Goulds, and Plants.

In the 1890s the developing technology of light steam engines and hulls designed to take advantage of them brought competition—in the United States from Charles Dell Mosher, like Nat Herreshoff a brilliant designer of both hulls and engines, and in England from Charles Parsons, who patented his steam-turbine engine in 1884. Mosher's *Norwood* of 1890, a 63-foot commuter for former Herreshoff customer Norman Munro, was timed at 30.5 mph—25 knots—and

Mosher's *Feiseen* of 1893 was slightly faster. *Feiseen*, a boat of international interest whose name meant "flying arrow" in Japanese, was sold to the Brazilian Navy. The Mosher-designed *Ellide* of 1896 was an 80-footer whose contract called for 30 mph and whose carefully measured speed trials recorded 40 mph. This was an unprecedented speed until Mosher's *Arrow*, designed and built for Charles R. Flint. *Arrow* was used for 18 years as a commuter under several owners, and was timed at 40.6 mph in 1901 and 45 mph in 1902.

While the Herreshoffs were designing and building fast steamers for millionaires and navies, across the sea in England the ultimate in steam power was being perfected. On June 27, 1897, a Naval Review at Spithead honored Queen Victoria's Diamond Jubilee and gathered about 27 miles of ships—170 vessels from the Home and Reserve Fleet, as well as ships of every foreign sea power. It was the largest gathering of marine experts in history.

Suddenly a 100-foot toothpick of a boat was seen racing down past ship after ship at the astonishing speed of 34 knots—39 mph. Picket boats, whose duty it was to keep the lines clear, could not begin to keep pace with the interloper. She was *Turbinia,* with the Honourable Charles Algernon Parsons at her helm. He was the inventor of not only the revolutionary 2,000-total-hp radial-flow steam turbines that drove the boat, but the designer of the slim steel hull. *Turbinia* was 100 feet long with a beam of 9 feet! She weighed 44-1/2 tons with three direct-drive turbines, each with a different steam-pressure stage, driving three shafts with three propellers on each shaft. Like Nat Herreshoff running rings around the legendary *Mary Powell* on the Hudson, this was a convincing demonstration. The future of Sir Charles's turbine engine was assured, and later and larger engines of this type drove the crack liners of the twentieth century—*Mauretania, Lusitania,* and the holder of the Atlantic Blue Riband, *Queen Mary I,* 31.6 knots on a transatlantic trip in 1931. Steam turbine engines quickly eclipsed reciprocating steam in fast military boats and civilian flyers. The first steam-turbine yacht in the United States was the aptly named *Revolution,* designed in 1902 by Charles L. Seabury using Curtis turbines.

But despite the turbine revolution there was a speed record left in the old technology of reciprocating steam. In any discussion of high-speed steam commuters one boat stands out. When her astounding speed was announced, it was compared to fast locomotives and the developing automobile. On a U.S. government course set up on the Hudson in the spring of 1902, a speed of 39.13 knots, or 45.06 mph, over the measured mile was achieved by the amazing *Arrow.* This 130' × 12'5" hull with two reciprocating engines of 3,500 or more horsepower each was designed by Charles Dell Mosher, a self-taught engineer who made a specialty of steam flyers with advanced hull shapes and light boilers. *Arrow* was commissioned by Charles R. Flint, a robber baron with interests in rubber, munitions, and shipping, to achieve world-record speeds—in fact, to surpass the five-year-old *Turbinia* record. She was built with sophistication and expense—$160,000—by Samuel Ayers and Sons of Nyack, New York, her hull of composite construction with thin double mahogany planking on frames that were steel below the water and aluminum

39

above. Her weight was only 67 tons. Mosher gave her a flat run aft so that she could absorb the full power of two quadruple-expansion steam engines of at least 3,500 hp without squatting.

Even with such sizable engines *Arrow* had some measure of interior accommodations, enough to keep her in service for nearly twenty years. She was a commuter for Charles Flint and later for J. Stuart Blackton, the flamboyant motorboat racer and founder of Vitagraph Pictures. From 1900 until now there are only a handful of high-speed boats that can compare with *Arrow*. It was not until 1911 that her speed was eclipsed, and even then it took an out-and-out raceboat to barely surpass it with a speed of 45.22 mph. *Dixie IV*, designed by Clinton Crane and powered by two state-of-the-art V8 gasoline engines designed by Clinton's brother, Henry, was faster than *Arrow* by 0.16 mph. Another commuter did not surpass *Arrow*'s speed until twenty years later when L. Gordon Hamersley's *Cigarette*, a 70-foot Gar Wood product, traveled at 50 mph, and it took all five of the 400-hp Wood/Liberty V-12s breathing hard and loudly to push this huge version of Gar Wood's smaller speedboats at such a pace.

CIGARETTE

Gordon Hamersley's Liberty-powered Gar Wood running easily on the Hudson River. Not much protection for the helmsman. Taken in the summer of 1923. A large bed-lounge is in place just forward of the deckhouse. Below were mostly engines and tanks.

CIGARETTE

With her five Liberties pounding, Cigarette is coming up fast to pass through the wake on the port side of Rosenfeld's photo boat. The extreme, sharp bow and narrow beam are evident in this shot. A great picture of a fast commuter in action!

The time between *Arrow*'s triumph of 1902 and such Roaring
Twenties flyers as Gordon Hamersley's fastest *Cigarettes* was a period of transition from long, slim steamers to smaller and lighter gas-
engine boats. The Herreshoffs still built steamers for the elite, the
fastest of which was the 20-plus-mph *Stroller*, built in 1901 for Gilbert
Rafferty of Pittsburgh, Pennsylvania, and Alexandria Bay, New York.
Matthew Borden went to the Herreshoffs in 1904 for his *Little Sovereign*, but switched allegiance to Charles L. Seabury in 1909 for *Little Sovereign II*, a steam flyer capable of 28 mph. In 1902 William K.
Vanderbilt had the famous *Tarantula* designed by Cox and King and
built by Yarrow in England with three Parsons steam turbines.

Peter Rouss commissioned his first *Winchester* in 1907, a 23-mph
steam commuter built by Robert Jacob in City Island, New York City,
to a design by Henry Gielow. And in 1909 and 1912 he went to Cox and
King for designs that became *Winchesters* II and III, both built by
Yarrow in England. The second *Winchester* had three Parsons steam

turbines in a 165′6″ hull that looked like a destroyer; the third *Winchester*, at 205 feet, was even more of a little ship, and reached 36 mph with two Yarrow steam turbines. The last and greatest of the *Winchesters*, all of them commuters, was *Winchester IV* of 1915, 225 feet and just a bit slower than III. She had two steam turbines in another steamship-style hull built in Maine by Bath Iron Works to a design by Cox and Stevens. *Winchester IV* gave thirty years of good service— to Peter Rouss during his lifetime, and then to Vincent Astor and to Cornelius Vanderbilt III.

One of the great commuting stories involves the second *Winchester* and the creation of Matthew Borden's "fast" *Sovereign*. One day in 1909 Matthew Borden aboard *Little Sovereign II* was passed on the way to work by Peter Rouss in his *Winchester II*. Borden ordered his captain not to dock in Manhattan but to head for the Harlem River and the premises of Charles L. Seabury and Gas Engine and Power Company, Consolidated, where he could contract for a faster yacht. The faster yacht was *Sovereign* of 1911, a 166-foot commuter that ultimately had three 2,000-hp Curtis steam turbines for a speed of more than 40 mph.

WINCHESTER IV
The fantastic Winchester *(the last one)—225 feet of commuter. Shown in 1936 on the New York Yacht Club annual cruise. She was then owned by Cornelius Vanderbilt III. Built in 1915, she served many notable yachtsmen for more than thirty years.*

Chapter Two

Petrochemicals and Planing Bottoms

A S THE TWENTIETH CENTURY ARRIVED, STEAM COMMUTERS WERE still the vehicles of choice for the nabobs of finance and industry. Naphtha engines were used for smaller boats such as launches. A launch was usually the biggest small boat carried aboard a large yacht, and the members of the American Yacht Club not only carried naphtha launches on their steam yachts but raced them on the weekends. A few of the naphtha boats were large, even though they kept the name "launch," notably AYC member Alfred Van Santvoord's 76-foot *Saranac*. Gasoline-engine development was in its infancy in 1900, although its promise had already been recognized on the waterfront. William Steinway, builder of mahogany pianos, took up the building of mahogany boats, with gasoline engines made in the United States under license from Daimler of Germany, in the 1890s, and other pioneers of "explosive" power were importing gasoline engines from Europe or building their own before 1900. During the 1901 boating season, nearly half the new boats reported under construction in *Rudder* magazine had gasoline power.

44

The Herreshoff Company preferred steam even though Nat had lost his license in 1888 when a boiler exploded during speed trials, killing a man. From 1858 to 1900 the Herreshoffs turned out more than two hundred powerboats, but beginning in the late 1880s the company's focus was increasingly on sailing yachts, from catboats to the great America's Cup defenders that raced between 1893 and 1920. Between 1900 and 1917, the Herreshoffs launched ninety-four powerboats, some of them elite vehicles for commuting. *Mirage*, the last Herreshoff 81-foot steam flyer, was built in 1910 for Cornelius Vanderbilt, and in 1917 J. P. Morgan, Jr.—"Jack" Morgan—ordered the 114-foot *Navette*, with twin Herreshoff steam engines, to carry him from Long Island to Wall Street.

As the Herreshoffs were shifting to sail, two significant boatyards were turning out steam commuters of note: the Lawley yard of Boston and Consolidated of New York.

NAVETTE
This enchanting Herreshoff commuter built in 1917 for J. P. Morgan, Jr. is living out the last years of her life, still barely afloat, in a backwater of Florida. One of the last of the great steam commuters, she may be nearly beyond saving. It is almost impossible to determine the private signal; however, it doesn't look like the star and crescent of Morgan père (red) and son (blue).

The Gas Engine and Power Company and Charles L. Seabury Company, Consolidated, which developed as large a shipbuilding operation as its name was long, had its beginnings in 1879 when Charles Lincoln Seabury, an enterprising draftsman who had worked for the Herreshoffs, set up a yard at Nyack, New York, to design and build steam yachts. According to L. Francis Herreshoff: "As a young man Mr. Seabury had worked in the boiler shop of the Herreshoff Manufacturing Company, and the first of his steam yacht engines were almost identical to those being made by that company when he was there."

In 1885, while Charles L. Seabury was building steam yachts and launches up the Hudson, what *Forest and Stream* magazine described as "a new gas engine" was making its debut on the Harlem River. This engine derived its power from the expansion of naphtha vapor upon its pistons—on the same principle as a steam engine. The new gas engine, invented by Frank W. Ofeldt, was the naphtha power plant that had a successful run in the 1890s, bridging the gap between steam and gasoline "explosive" engines. Even though it boiled and vaporized its fuel, the naphtha engine hardly ever exploded, and its success was assured because a naphtha boat could be run without a licensed steam engineer aboard. Boiling water required a license; boiling a volatile petrochemical did not. The Gas Engine and Power Company was soon recognized as the builder of "the only naptha launch," and its products were in service all over the world.

The original shop on the Harlem River, at 131st Street and Brook Avenue, was soon outgrown, and in 1887 the company moved to larger premises at Morris Dock, later known as Morris Heights, also along the Harlem River in the Bronx. In 1890 the Gas Engine and Power Company built two hundred of their popular naphtha launches; they were high technology for their brief time—quick to fire up, relatively unfussy in operation, and lighter than the steam launches that had previously been carried aboard the big steam yachts.

In 1896 a consolidation between the Gas Engine and Power Company and Charles L. Seabury and Company was arranged, whereby the latter company moved from Nyack to Morris Heights. This brought together some of the best powerboat technology of the time—steam, naphtha, and, soon enough, gasoline engines. Additional property was purchased, new buildings were put up, and the latest machinery and tools for boat- and engine-building were installed. The company continued—according to their forty-page catalog of 1919 —"on an increasing scale, the construction of yachts and launches, and their propelling machinery, and turned out the finest craft built in this country."

Consolidated signed its first contract with the U.S. Navy in 1897 for the design, construction, and powering of one of the first of the world's torpedo-boat destroyers, known as the "Bailey" class. This early "destroyer" was renowned in naval circles all over the world, and for several years had the honor of being the fastest ship in the navy. Two other naval vessels, the destroyer *Stewart* and the torpedo boat *Wilkes,* were built soon after, and the company became an important government contractor, building steam launches, lifeboats, engines and boilers, as well as the gunboats *Dubuque* and *Paducah.*

In 1903 Consolidated began building its first gasoline marine engine, giving it the name Speedway for the then-famous wide road on the other side of the Harlem River where the rich and famous brought their carriages and later their motorcars to see and to be seen at speed. The Consolidated Speedway gasoline engine was a fine piece of machinery, a compact, easily managed power plant for its time, and the beginning of the company's reputation for elegant, fast, reliable gas-engine boats, many of them commuters. Consolidated's first gasoline-powered yacht was a 67-footer built in 1903.

Also in 1903 the 111-foot *Niagara IV* was built for Howard Gould. In 1905 the 120-foot *Vitesse,* with two 3-cylinder Speedway gas engines for close to 30 mph, was built for General Brayton Ives. In 1911 the famous *Sovereign III*—the fast *Sovereign*—was built for Matthew C. D. Borden after his losing contest with Peter Rouss and his second *Winchester.* She was a 166-foot steamer with three turbine engines for 40-plus mph. In 1912 Consolidated built *Dark Island* for F. G. Bourne, a 60-foot Thousand Islands commuter with a single Speedway gas engine that gave her more than 20 mph. Although Consolidated stayed with steam in the years before World War I—and with the fast *Sovereign* produced one of the great ones—gasoline engines were evolving as more powerful units, and the demand grew for gasoline-powered auto boats, express cruisers for exhilarating recreation, and especially for fast commuters which the company soon produced in large numbers. Consolidated catalogs in these years, displaying all of its wares from engines to standard-model boats to such chandlery items as stoves and deck fittings, were as bulky as forty pages or more. In its heyday, from roughly 1900 to 1930, Consolidated was possibly the largest custom yacht-building operation in the world.

During World War I the company offered its entire resources to the U.S. Navy. Alongside the naval vessels abuilding, a number of Consolidated customers' yachts were converted to coastal patrol craft. Government contracts included five 1,000-ton steel seagoing minesweepers and 175 flying-boat hulls built of wood by the yard's small-boat division.

After the war, as noted in the company's 1919 catalog, "Consolidated was building the largest and finest American steam yachts, gasoline yachts, commuters, house boats, motor cruisers, open launches, speed launches, runabouts, yacht tenders and various other types." Consolidated designed and built the hulls and fitted them with its own power plants, electrical equipment, plumbing, upholstery, the unique and ornate Speedway stoves, all the furnishings that made a Consolidated ready-to-go in every detail.

The Consolidated yard was huge, and its resources were up-to-the-minute. A total of thirteen ways made possible the launching of vessels to 300 feet, and these ultimately included not only big yachts but small freighters. By 1907 the company was using its own measured test course laid out on one of the canals off the Harlem River. It was here that Clinton Crane ran progressive speed trials that led to more accurate calculations and tables for naval architecture and gave Crane, a man who designed some of the fastest boats in the world, part of his apprenticeship.

Although Charles Lincoln Seabury was the primary influence on

Consolidated in its first decades, as time and success went on the company attracted other astute businessmen and investors. The Consolidated board of directors became a veritable Who's Who of the yachting business world of the 1920s and 1930s, and leaders in other lines of business—men in the market for fast yachts—were attracted to Consolidated as customers. The Speedway series of commuters were considered by many yachtsmen the finest express yachts of their time.

North of Cape Cod, another yacht builder whose history and influence paralleled that of Consolidated was making its mark on steam and later gasoline flyers—the Lawley yard of Boston. George Frederick Lawley worked for his father, another George who had come to Boston from England in 1851, and in 1866 father and son laid the keel for their first yacht in Scituate, on Boston's South Shore. Eight years later members of the Boston Yacht Club induced the Lawleys to move to South Boston, where the two great America's Cup defenders *Puritan* and *Mayflower* were built in 1885 and 1886. George F. Lawley and Son became one of the nation's largest yacht builders between 1880 and 1910, and in that year the Lawley plant was moved to larger premises across Dorchester Bay at Neponset where the America's Cup defense contender *Vanitie* and other yachts, power and sail, large and small, were built.

One of the Lawley yard's first express yacht/commuters was *Cigarette*, a 126-foot A. Loring Swasey design similar to his World War I subchasers. She was a 22-knot, twin-engine steam commuter built for William H. Ames in 1905. This *Cigarette*—likely the first of all the fast boats of that name—express cruisers, commuters, at least one rumrunner, and in our own time Don Aronow's famous offshore racer—was used by the U.S. Navy in World War I and then went to Barron Collier as *Pocantino* in 1921. Other well-known Lawley express-commuters of the 1900–1920 era were *Welcome*, a 72-footer built in 1910, and *Gem*, a 164-footer built in 1913. *Gem*, designed by Cox and Stevens, was the last Lawley-built steam commuter and served the navy in World War I for experiments with submarine detection. Although the Lawley yard was known for traditional types,

49

sail and power, they undertook the building of two very advanced gas-engine boats in 1915 and 1916 designed by the forward-thinking William Hand, Jr. In 1915, one of Hand's first commuter designs, *Raccoon*, was built for Chester Bliss. This 50′ × 10″ express cruiser ran without fuss at 25 mph powered by two 250-hp Van Blerck sixes. She was faster than the vaunted Consolidated 115-foot steam commuter *Vivace*. In 1916 the Lawley yard built the Hand-designed *Countess*, a fast boat for the designer himself. She was a 40-footer with a single 175-hp Van Blerck gas engine for 30 mph. Both boats were the commuting future—relatively light, hard-chine, V-bottom hulls with gasoline engines.

Along with Herreshoff, Lawley, and Consolidated, Yarrow of torpedo-boat fame in England built commuters for American owners in the new century, notably the notorious *Tarantula*. This 153-foot destroyer-type flyer was built in 1902, and when brought over to the U.S. by William K. Vanderbilt created a minor sensation because of the damage caused by her wake while running at speed on the East and Harlem rivers. There were no local marine patrols in those days, nor indeed much marine regulation beyond the Rules of the Road, but a court case was decided against *Tarantula,* making her owner responsible for the damage of his vessel's wake. Some early photos show a deck gun mounted on *Tarantula'*s stern. Was this for protection from wake-damage victims?

Yarrow Ltd. became better known in the United States when the awesome *Winchesters* II and III, mentioned earlier, were built for Peter Winchester Rouss, a New York department-store owner who devoted much of his time and money to installing lavish Civil War memorials in selected cities. Peter Winchester devoted himself with equal fervor to another hobby—fast destroyer-type commuter yachts, each one larger and faster than its predecessor. The last *Winchester* evidently satisfied his need for transportation of naval proportions, as he commuted from Long Island to Manhattan in her for a dozen years and wreaked daily havoc on the docks and small boats along his route. In Peter Winchester Rouss's lifetime he owned a total of 737 feet of commuters. This seems to be something of a record.

TARANTULA

The Vanderbilt commuter of an earlier age, the notorious torpedo-boat type Tarantula. The crew is getting ready to launch the starboard deck boat. Notice the sizable deck gun aft. With her nine propellers (three on each shaft), her wake caused a famous lawsuit. She was powered by three Parsons steam turbines.

The first *Winchester* was designed by Henry Gielow and was built in 1907 at Robert Jacob's yard in City Island, the Bronx. *Winchester I* was 141'5" long with a beam of 15'5", and she approached 20 knots with twin reciprocating steam engines. Peter used her for two seasons, but soon got the urge for something larger and faster. He sold her to A. G. Vanderbilt in 1909 and promptly commissioned Cox and King of New York to design a larger—165'6" × 15'6"—*Winchester II*. This one was destroyer-looking and powered by three Parsons steam turbines. She was an improvement over *Winchester I*—her 2500 hp pushed her smoothly to 25 knots. Peter was now getting into the spirit of these huge, rapid machines, and he sold *Winchester II* to Irving Cox and Company in 1912 and placed an order for his third *Winchester*—like II to be built and turbine-powered by Yarrow. Cox and King (by then Cox and Stevens) was asked to design something similar to the second *Winchester,* but with a dining saloon and capable of withstanding some 7,000 hp. At 205 feet and 32 knots she carried an owner's stateroom and in a pinch slept two more in single staterooms that shared a small head. In today's go-fast cruisers of 40 feet and over, a stateroom without its own adjacent gold-fixtured head is considered almost camping out.

Peter Rouss liked this third *Winchester* a little better, but again was moved to visit Cox and Stevens in 1915 to augment his one-vessel, one-man navy with a new *Winchester* 20 feet longer. For a time he had a two-vessel navy while he kept the previous *Winchester* in commission. This new boat was the greatest of the *Winchesters,* and Peter Rouss used her to travel to his mercantile offices in Manhattan from the 52-acre estate near Oyster Bay that he inherited from his father. She was famous in the 1920s for her size, her speed, and the damage caused by her wake. Although *Winchester IV* was 225 feet long with a 21-foot beam, she had the same 7,000 hp, about as much as one would want in a private destroyer. She also had the same meager accommodations as III. Even so she must have been a very satisfying vessel; she was owned at various times by the U.S. Navy (on loan from Peter Rouss during World War I); by Vincent Astor, who bought her in 1928; by Cornelius Vanderbilt III, who became her owner in

1930; and by the Canadian Navy in World War II. During his later years General Vanderbilt lived aboard her at the Municipal Docks in downtown Miami while his family, definite non-nautical people, lived in splendor at their estate in Newport. The devastating Florida hurricane of '35 was no threat to *Winchester*—she rode it out offshore. Vanderbilt's dockage and maintenance costs in Miami were a mere $7,000 a month for this half-size dreadnought that became the Armed Yacht *Renard,* His Majesty's Canadian Ship, during World War II. These payments usually came from Mr. Vanderbilt's mother, as did the annual five-figure commissioning checks. Vanderbilt in later years led a quiet life, and he died aboard *Winchester IV* in 1942. She was still seen around Miami in the 1950s, and was last listed in *Lloyd's* in 1956 under the ownership of the Margaree Steamship Company, with London as her port of registry.

Outstanding steam commuters like Charles Flint's *Arrow,* W. K. Vanderbilt's *Tarantula,* Matthew Borden's "fast" *Sovereign,* Jack Morgan's *Navette,* and all of the *Winchesters,* were the best of the second generation of commuter yachts—the first generation being slow but sumptuous steam vehicles like H. W. Schneider's *Esperance,* J. P. Morgan's steam launch *Louisa,* and all the Morgan *Corsairs.* This second generation brought speed to the game, and in the new century the pursuit of speed brought gasoline engines and planing bottoms to powerboats that ranged from raceboats to rumboats to commuters.

The origins of the gasoline engine go back to experimental work by Dr. Nikolaus August Otto, born in Prussia in 1832. Otto developed his first "explosive" engine, which was not successful, as early as 1863. Soon enough he was fortunate to meet a skillful designer of machinery in Cologne, Eugen Langen, who made better use of Otto's ideas, and by the time of the 1876 Paris Exposition some five thousand Otto-Langen engines had been sold. This was a tall, awkward engine of .86 horsepower that ran on illuminating gas, not the sublime 4-stroke-cycle engine that changed the world. But within that year the great 4-stroke principle—intake, compression/ignition, power, exhaust—had been thought out by Otto and he began licensing worldwide in 1878 on patents granted in 1877.

By 1878 the Otto 4-stroke-cycle "gas-o-lene" engine was being sold in the United States largely due to a visit by an engineer from the Otto works, Wilhelm Maybach. The enterprising Maybach and Gottlieb Daimler later set up their own firm to produce a new "high-speed" 4-cycle engine, and in 1886 they installed one in a boat. The year before, Clark Sintz of Grand Rapids, one of the first of the midwestern motorheads who would transform American transportation, had demonstrated a 2-cycle engine in a small boat up in Michigan. His Sintz Gas Engine Company built an American version of the 2-cycle engine that had been perfected in the late 1870s by the Scotsman Dugald Clerk, and seems to have been one of the first U.S. builders of gasoline engines, 2-cycle and 4-cycle, licensed and unlicensed, for farms, factories, boats, and soon enough for horseless carriages.

From 1891 to 1897 the Steinway Piano Company of New York built Daimler gasoline engines and boats to accommodate them, and in 1895, when Dr. Otto's and Dugald Clerk's patent rights ran out, gasoline-engine builders appeared everywhere, especially on the world's waterfronts. Speedboats were not far behind. In 1900 the first race for *canots automobiles* took place on the Seine as part of the Paris Universal Exposition. Thus began the "autoboat" craze that influenced the future of fast motorboating in America and Europe for years to come. The Europeans were a little more advanced in gas-engine technology at the turn of the century, with such worthy contemporaries as Daimler (by then renamed Mercedes), Napier, F.I.A.T., Mors, Darracq, Peugeot, Delahaye, Panhard et Levassor. In America, gas-engine builders were getting into the fray with Chadwick, Simplex, Olds, Standard, Wolverine, Winton and others delivering more powerful and sometimes more reliable engines than the Europeans.

By 1903 Consolidated began building their Speedway gasoline engines, and in that same year Carl and Eugene Riotte put their awesome Standard engine into the 60-foot speedboat of the same name. *Standard*, capable of more than 30 mph, would have made a fine commuter with her 110-hp, 3,016-cubic-inch, 3200-pound engine. The first New York Motor Boat Show opened in 1905 with many famous names in attendance—Fay and Bowen, Speedway, Standard, Bridge-port, Victor, Buffalo, Globe, Lozier, Sterling, Murray and Tregurtha—and in 1905 the May issue of *Rudder* magazine carried advertising for no fewer than sixty-three builders of gasoline marine engines. Things were moving along with the speed of *canots automobiles.*

The marine gas engines used in powerboats during the first twenty-five years—roughly 1890 to 1915—were inconsistent in quality and reliability, although some engines, such as those from Kermath, Sterling, Scripps, Standard, and Van Blerck, represented some of the best engineering practice of the day. They were priced accordingly. The 100-hp Scripps of 1911 was priced at $3,500, more than the cost of some luxury automobiles. In 1914, the Van Blerck Motor Company of Monroe, Michigan, advertised its E-8 Special, a high-speed model developing up to 220 hp, for $2,420. The Scripps, Van Blerck, and other premium engines were considered "high-speed" marine power—they were able to run at more than 1,300 rpm. Cylinder bores ran 5 to 7 inches with strokes of 6 to 8 inches.

There were also power limitations, which would later be solved by the aircraft engines of World War I, but solved first in a little boat-shop in Huntington, Long Island, by building two big engines from scratch, a good example of the often-brilliant ad hoc engineering of the time. In the New Boat Shop of William Atkin and Cot Wheeler, the power needs of a 115′ × 13′ commuter called *Cabrilla* could not be met by any existing marine engine in 1914, so Atkin designed two huge 750-hp V8s and Wheeler built them. Billy Atkin would make his reputation as a journalist and yacht designer, but he seems to have been able to design anything. His two V8s had 8-inch cylinder bores and 14-inch strokes and weighed 5,500 pounds each. They pushed *Cabrilla,* a displacement-hull commuter built for coal and zinc magnate August Heckscher, to 30 mph.

Bore, stroke, rpm, and weight are important here because before World War I, and even up through the 1920s, the constraints imposed by the fuels of the day were formidable. Many engine builders used twin ignition—two spark plugs per cylinder. This looked good in the ads and suggested sophistication, but two plugs per cylinder helped get the fires going. Compression ratios could not be raised too high because at the time there were no anti-knock ingredients in motor fuels. Tetraethyl lead was not mixed into gasoline until 1924, and the octane scale for gasoline was not devised until 1926. Big changes in fuel didn't arrive until the aircraft-engine developments of the late 1930s.

Aircraft-engine development became an important factor in the progress of all gasoline engines during World War I, and progress was rapid in engine design, metallurgy, horsepower-to-weight ratios. At first rotary engines—with the entire engine rotating along with the propeller—were used by both sides. These were all constant-speed, air-cooled engines. The only way the intrepid pilot could control the speed of the engine was by the interrupt button on the joystick which cut off the fire from the ignition. Later more than one button was used, cutting off the fire from a few of the cylinders to give somewhat more control of the revs. The intricacies of the carburetor were considered too fussy for engine control in the air. As these rotary engines became heavier in the quest for more speed and a greater rate of climb they almost became flying gyroscopes.

The great aircraft genius Anthony Fokker saw the possibilities of in-line water-cooled engines for quicker and more maneuverable fighter aircraft, and his astute choice was the 160-hp, water-cooled, in-line 6-cylinder Mercedes engine of Daimler Motoren Gesellschaft. Around this engine he designed the magical Fokker D-VII. About a thousand of these planes were built by the time of the Armistice, and Fokker's D-VII was paid the signal honor of being the only German airplane named as booty by the Allies in the surrender terms.

By 1917 the Allies had only one airplane capable of dueling successfully with the Fokker D-VII—the Hispano-Suiza–powered S.P.A.D., the famous hat-in-the-ring plane of Eddie Rickenbacker and the French aces Fonck and Guynemer. This engine designed by a young Swiss engineer, Mark Birkigt, was a curiously advanced conception for its time—overhead cams, one-piece aluminum block with screwed-in cylinder liners, dual ignition with cam-driven magnetos, forced lubrication. By the end of 1917, the Wright-Martin Corporation of New Brunswick, New Jersey, was building 150-hp, 200-hp and 300-hp Hispano-Suiza engines under license. Unfortunately, the celebrated Liberty engine, a product of the United States of America Standard Aircraft Engine Company, and supposedly designed in six days in a Washington, D.C., hotel room, was almost too late to have an impact on the war. But more than twenty thousand of these 400-hp water-cooled V-12 engines were built and were available as surplus, in whole and in part, after the Armistice.

When the twenties began to roar, the surplus 300-hp Wright-Hispanos could be had complete with spare parts for about $350, and the mighty Liberty V-12s could be bought for around $2,000—crated and pickled, and provided with tools and an instruction manual. These were ideal engines for big, fast boats, and they found their way into Gold Cup raceboats, rumrunners, and the great express yachts and commuters of the 1920s. Especially the Liberty. The Hisso, although a rugged engine for the time, was at about its reliable limit at 300 hp. The Liberty, however, was able to be tweaked from its original 400 hp to more than 600 hp, a challenge happily met by various marine-engine companies—Grant, Capitol, Gar Wood, Johnson, Lee, Vimalert, and Van Blerck among them.

During the twenty-odd years when gasoline engines were becoming faster and lighter, hulls were doing the same. The Herreshoff, Consolidated, Yarrow, and Lawley flyers of the steam era were long, slender displacement hulls built on a rather large scale to allow for ponderous steam machinery and its attendant supply of coal, along with relatively large crews to run the engines, shovel the coal, and attend to the food and booze requirements of cruising or commuting passengers. The power plant took up the best part of the yacht amidships, and all the owner usually got was the deck and the after part of the hull. Steam-vessel designers normally followed the rules, put in a certain amount of power and went so fast—usually about 10 knots. If the owner wanted higher speed, the hull size was increased to accommodate a larger power plant and that was the end of it. The power yachtsman of a hundred years ago had to put up with boats

BLACK WATCH

This scout-patrol type commuter by Tams, Lemoine and Crane was built in 1917. Notice the fake stack and the reverse sheer—she is not hogged. The forward engine hatch seems to be uncovered giving access to the single Duesenberg engine. A long-forgotten amusement park is abandoned on Morris Heights along the Harlem River.

COUNTESS

William Hand's V-bottom express cruiser-commuter, a state-of-the-art design that changed the thinking of many naval architects and established records before 1920.

GET THERE

Designed by Tams, Lemoine and Crane during World War I, and built at City Island, New York City, by Wood and McClure, she was powered by two Ford-Packard 12-cylinder engines forward of the helm. She was owned by Edsel Ford, and later named Greyhound.

that were uncomfortable, unseaworthy by current standards, and furnished with meager accommodations on a given length. Variation between one good design and another was hardly visible, and differences in speed with the same power were insignificant.

Then, in the early part of the twentieth century, when far-lighter gasoline marine engines began to drive the design of power yachts, a few pioneers, experimenting with V-bottom hulls and decreased displacement, suddenly found that very much higher speeds could be obtained if the hull were forced on top of the water. This was not a new idea. Any designer or experimenter, towing a model at increasing speed, would have noticed that at a certain point of speed increase the little hull would lift out of its hole in the water, ride up and over its bow wave, and move along with a sudden decrease in resistance. This worked best if the model had a flat rather than a round bottom. As far back as 1872, the first planing form was patented by the Reverend C. M. Ramus, an English clergyman who had a curious interest in speed on the water. His idea was a rectangular, two-stepped, almost flat-bottomed hull form. He even developed, in model and principle, something like a three-point hydroplane. But the lack of suitable lightweight power doomed this device and a later flat-bottomed speedboat hull conceived by a Frenchman in 1887. Charles Dell Mosher's steam flyers of the 1890s did better. Semi-planing, they gained some lift from relatively flat V-shaped after sections that may have been designed to resist the brutal torque of their engines and propellers.

The planing bottom evolved in the first decade of the twentieth century, and it evolved quickly and in several places, with creative work done by French sportsmen whose 10′ × 5′ *hydro-glisseurs* zipped along the Seine at 15 mph in 1905; by Alfred Luders of Stamford, Connecticut, who built a one-step hydroplane in 1907; by John Hacker of Detroit, whose experiments with flat-section planing hulls have been reported as early as 1901; by William Henry Fauber, a Chicago engineer living in France whose patent for a hydroplane with eight steps in its shallow-V bottom was granted in 1908; by S. E. Saunders of Cowes, England, who followed Fauber's patent ideas to produce the amazing 50-knot *Maple Leaf IV* in 1912; by William Hand of New Bedford, Massachusetts, whose experiments with V-bottom launches began in 1903 and produced a 38-foot cruiser called *Flyaway III* in 1914 that moved smartly along in coastal chop at 20 mph with a 100-hp Van Blerck engine. Hand's two Lawley-built commuter designs, *Raccoon* and *Countess,* followed the influential *Flyaway* in 1915 and 1916.

The principles of planing were well-known and well-established when World War I brought an apparent need for fast powerboats to patrol the U.S. East Coast, and in Europe brought forth the 50- and 69-foot Italian MAS boats and England's 40- and 55-foot CMBs. Both the 30-knot Italian boats and the 37-knot British boats were a new naval weapon, able to sink big ships with self-propelled torpedos, making lightning raids on enemy harbors and then speeding away. Most significantly, they were big planing boats with lightweight gasoline engines—a type that would appear in the 1920s as rumboats, express yachts, and the fastest of the commuters. The gasoline engine and the planing bottom had come a long way from the French *hydroglisseurs* of 1905 and the planing raceboats of the prewar years.

On these shores during World War I, civilian express cruisers served the military in a burst of patriotic speedboating that caused the founding of the U.S. Power Squadrons, saw patrol boats built by the government and by yachtsmen, and even made use of steam yachts for anti-submarine scouting and other duty. In late 1915, while serving as acting secretary of the navy, Franklin D. Roosevelt announced a plan to create a fifty-thousand-man national reserve, made up largely of civilian volunteers, to supplement existing state naval militias. This called for suitable motorboats to be developed and built. The government would help in cooperation with a power-yachting community eager to play navy and protect America from the plausible threat of Hun submarines. Volunteer patrol squadrons were formed, notably those led by Roger Upton in Boston and Stewart Davis in Southampton, Long Island, and plans were made for government-built patrol vessels. In 1916 some scout types were built by patriotic yachtsmen—among them Vanderbilt's Patrol Boat 8, a 72-

SUBCHASER NUMBER 317
*One of the 110-foot coastal
patrol subchasers that served
during World War I and were
later used during Prohibition.
An inexpensive but robust
wooden craft powered by
three Standard 200 hp
engines. One of the great A.
Loring Swasey designs but not
fast enough at 16–18 knots to
be effective against the fast
rumboats.*

footer designed by A. Loring Swasey; Nat Ayer's 45′9″ *Lynx* (SP-2),
built by Lawley; and Ralph Pulitzer's 71-foot *Mystery,* an exciting 24-
knot boat built by Luders and powered by two Duesenberg gasoline
engines of 400 hp each.

The General Board of the Navy soon established design charac-
teristics applicable to such vessels, and even conducted a design contest for fast—over 16 knots—boats to be government-built. Loring
Swasey won the competition with a 45-footer, although a 66-foot
design from Luders was considered a better boat, especially in lumpy
conditions. By 1917, boards were established for motorboat inspection in Boston, Newport, New York, Philadelphia, Norfolk, Charles-
ton, Key West, Pensacola, New Orleans, San Francisco, Bremerton,
and at the Great Lakes Naval Training Station.

Despite what might seem to be a lot of activity, the U.S. Navy built

only five 40-foot patrol boats before hostilities ceased, although 550 19-knot patrol and torpedo vessels of 75 and 110 feet were built in 1915 and 1916 by Elco of Bayonne, New Jersey, for the British, and more than 400 110-foot subchasers were built by a variety of yards for the U.S. Navy before 1920. But during the war, and continuing for a few years after at a greater rate, quite a few express yachts of the scout and torpedo types, having a decidedly sinister look about them, were designed and built for patriotic yachtsmen. Long, low-profile, high-powered and fast, both of rounded and hard-chine designs, and some with deck guns indicated on their construction drawings, these boats could be converted with minimum revision into the fast commuters of the Roaring Twenties. Some of them were. More significantly, their technology of light weight relative to the steamers that had served commuting yachtsmen for forty years, planing hull forms, high-speed gasoline engines of rapidly growing horsepower, and sheer go-fast glamor, was in place. And the Roaring Twenties were their time.

Chapter Three

The Roaring Commuters

A DECADE OF EXCITEMENT AND EXCESS—ALMOST EXACTLY DEFINED by the onset of Prohibition in the United States and the beginning of the Great Depression—the 1920s broke with the mores and mechanical habits of the nineteenth century and suddenly brought everything from airplane rides to stock speculation to wild nights in speakeasies to people whose lives had been slower and less adventurous only a few years before. On the waterfront, the "autoboats" of the previous two decades became the "speedboats" built by Chris-Craft, Gar Wood, John Hacker, and others—boats sold from auto-style showrooms and capable of as much as 40 mph thanks to the aircraft engines developed during World War I. And the patrol-boat types commissioned by patriotic yachtsmen in reaction to the German-submarine scare, along with lesser express cruisers built along the lines of William Hand's V-bottom boats, became the commuting vehicles of this great decade of yachts in a hurry. As journalist and yacht designer Weston Farmer wrote of the people and powerboats of the 1920s: "The exciting speeds of these boats entranced a new boating public which had left city and farm during WWI to see how things were done in Gay Paree—which generally was faster."

Speed on the water was not only exhilarating in the 1920s, it was practical for gentlemen commuting. The trip to and from work could be made with dispatch, without the bother of catching a train or being driven on two-lane roads clogged in the 1920s by something new—traffic—a result of the success of the automobile. Nearly 850,000 cars were built in the United States in 1920 alone. As the already-quoted writer of an ad for Consolidated's 1920s commuter yachts noted: "Commuting—in its newest sense—by water—has arrived. Down the bay, up the river, in from outside—you see these fleet, rakish, swagger-looking craft speeding hundreds of busy executives to downtown offices refreshed and eager for a great day's work . . ."

Commuter yachts were never a widespread phenomenon—they depended, obviously, on waterway links between home and office, and in cities with suitable waterways commuting by boat seems to have been influenced by local custom and perhaps by the ease with which a leader of his city's finance or industry could travel to work by other means. Los Angeles and San Francisco never developed much in the way of commuter fleets—the former because it had few suitable waterways and perhaps because its richer working citizens lived in town, the latter because—despite vexing commutes by bridge and ferry—the East Coast phenomenon of commuting by boat did not seem to arrive, our ad writer's assurances notwithstanding. In Phoenix and Dallas, of course, nobody commuted by boat. But in Chicago and Boston, cities with suburbs along the water, boat commuting never developed as fully as it did in New York and Detroit. Boston and Chicago were conservative cities, and it may be that local custom did not encourage the ostentation of travel by yacht to a workday of otherwise Puritan-ethic business. Other waterfront cities come to mind—Portland in Maine and Oregon, Cincinnati, Louisville, St. Louis, Memphis, New Orleans, Philadelphia, Jacksonville, Tampa-St. Petersburg, Mobile, San Diego, Seattle, even

Minneapolis-St. Paul. None of these cities seem to have taken to yacht commuting—as far as we can determine. Nor was there much yacht commuting in Miami and Miami Beach—booming with business in the 1920s. It may be that Florida cities had more commuting in their glory days than we can trace—small-boat commuting, say, between Coconut Grove and downtown Miami or between Bradenton and St. Pete. Warm weather and calm, inviting open water between home and office would have made such a thing attractive—but launches and runabouts would have been the vehicles rather than the big commuter yachts that served the purpose in the North.

New York was the great commuting city, with docks for visiting yachts maintained in the 1920s by the New York Yacht Club, the Montauk Yacht Club, and the Columbia Yacht Club, and with perhaps eighty commuters dashing into town by 1927, when the *New York Times* reported that "the Marchioness of Queensberry recently called the daily arrival of local plutocrats at the New York Yacht Club landing one of the greatest sights of the city."

During the twenties, builders of express yachts—Consolidated, Luders, the Purdy brothers, Gar Wood—began to specialize in commuters, and late in the decade stock boats for commuting came along from Chris-Craft, Robinson, Huckins, Hacker, and American Car and Foundry (acf). These were in addition to custom boats from such design firms as Tams and King, John H. Wells and Company, and Eldredge-McInnis. Perhaps the most elegant of the "semi-stock" commuters of the twenties and early thirties were Consolidated's Speedway series.

The first of the unbroken-sheerline Consolidated Speedway commuters was the 60-foot *Dark Island*, built in 1912 for Frederick G. Bourne of New York City and Dark Island, Chippewa Bay, in the Thousand Islands. *Dark Island* was a 22-mph flyer with low trunk cabins and a large, covered cockpit aft. The unprotected helmsman sat atop the forward trunk behind a bus-type steering wheel. This boat's original power plant was one of Consolidated's straight-six Speedway engines of 210 hp, 8-inch bore and stroke, a big, reliable piece of machinery longer than the average three-cushion sofa and produced

*The interior of the large
machine shop at the
Consolidated works in the
1920s. The Speedway engine
cylinder heads, blocks, and
pistons can be seen. This was
one of the largest pleasure-
boat operations of all time and
was located on the Harlem
River in New York City.*

by Consolidated for seventeen years. *Dark Island* served the Bourne family and three subsequent owners in the Northeast, and in about 1940 was brought to Florida where she was last listed in *Lloyd's* in 1962. With proper care, a Consolidated Speedway commuter would serve her owners well for fifty years.

In 1922 Consolidated designed and built a fast 62-foot cruiser along *Dark Island*'s lines for Julius Fleishmann of New York. *Whirlwind* was powered by two new Consolidated sixes—high-speed, dual-valve Speedway engines that developed 300 hp and drove *Whirlwind* at 30 mph. In spite of two big engines, she had spacious owners' quarters with built-in berths, full galley, enclosed head, and a sizeable deckhouse with control station. She was fitted with other amenities such as a radio, forward cockpit, cedar closets, a revolutionary new floor covering called linoleum, and crew quarters aft of the engine room. With her unbroken sheerline, 10′2″ beam, and graceful profile, *Whirlwind* was much admired not only for speed but for her sea-keeping qualities when making outside runs and overnight trips.

Consolidated built *Pauline M,* a similar vessel, in 1922 for Tom

PAULINE M

*One of the first commuters of the
Consolidated Speedway series. The
unbroken sheerline and forward cockpit
are noticeable. She is flying the owner's
private signal and the burgee of the
American (New York), Yacht Club.*

SCARAMOUCHE

*A gull's-eye view of Scaramouche,
another of the Consolidated Speedway
commuter series. In this picture at the
Yale–Harvard race in 1924, the narrow
beam of this 1923, 62-foot craft is noticeable. She is similar to Pauline M but
with a flying bridge.*

Howell. She used the same Speedway engines and was 57′ × 10′ with the same good looks and good behavior. *Pauline M* was followed by *Scaramouche,* a graceful Thoroughbred launched in 1923. *Scaramouche* was owned by H. N. Slater and was used for northern cruising and commuting in the summers, running to Florida in the winters. She was a celebrated traveler with the ability to sustain a speed of 30 mph. Another 1923 Speedway commuter was *Miss Asia* (ex-*Bing*)—a now-restored boat that joined the fleet of Commuters '91, the second gathering of surviving commuters and an event that will be described in some detail in later pages. Other notable Consolidated Speedway products of the twenties were *Escapade,* a 61-footer launched in 1925; *Ragtime* (ex-*Julie M*), a 64-footer launched in 1928; and *Red Wing, Mohican,* and *Dolphin,* 66-foot yachts built in 1929. *Ragtime* was also part of the Commuters '91 fleet on Long Island Sound, and joined Commuters '89 for a cruise from the Thousand Islands to Ottawa.

These exceptionally fast, comfortable cruisers with Speedway gas engines, and with similar sweeping-sheerline profiles, were built until the latter 1930s. One or two were said to be designed by John Hacker; however, as far as can be determined the entire Speedway commuter series was an in-house effort that produced semi-stock models with the owner's choice of arrangements on deck and below. Excellent examples of Consolidated workmanship, they were usually put to steady and sometimes demanding use by their owners, and some saw government service during World War II as patrol boats. Their round-bottom, penetrating hulls with sharp entry were lightly built for their day but proved to be extremely rugged. *Miss Asia, Ragtime, Mohican,* and *Dolphin* are still in commission every boating season, and *Mohican* did not need an automatic bilge pump until 1990. Consolidated built similar express yachts to plans by outside designers, notably *Phoenix,* a lovely 65′8″ Sparkman and Stephens creation built by Consolidated in 1937. I remember seeing her in the 1960s always going somewhere—once side-towing a 31-foot Bertram at a good clip down the New River in Fort Lauderdale. She is still in commission in California waters as *Old Age.* Another Speedway look-

69

BING (MISS ASIA)

This picture was taken in 1934 and shows this well-known commuter in her earlier configuration without the enclosed bridge. She is on her way to the Harvard–Yale boat races and is flying large Yale faculty flags, the owner's private signal, and the New York Yacht Club burgee.

JULIE M II (RAGTIME)

One of the later series of the Speedway commuters by Consolidated. Now appropriately named Ragtime, she has been completely rebuilt and repowered with diesels. Sporting a glossy black hull and a flying bridge, she is a stunning commuter.

PHOENIX

An attractive Sparkman and Stephens design of the late 1930s, built by Consolidated for Major Bowes of the radio "Amateur Hour" fame. Shown in 1937, flying the Burgee of the Dauntless (Connecticut) Club. She is similar in design to the Herreshoff-built Avoca.

MOHICAN

The most original of all the Consolidated Speedway series of commuters in existence, shown here shortly after she was commissioned in 1929. Owned by the Madsen family, she is being slowly restored and looks the same today.

NASHIRA

First of the high-speed, houseboat-type commuters by Consolidated, she ran between Massachusetts and New York City in the 1920s. She was one of five of the V-12 Typhoon-powered, 30-mph houseboats, and is shown here flying the Hoyt private signal and the NYYC burgee.

alike was *Avoca,* designed by Sparkman and Stephens and built for E. E. Dickinson in 1939 by the Herreshoff yard.

While not part of the Speedway series of commuters, a novel type the company described as a fast houseboat-cruiser was developed by Consolidated in the mid-1920s. At least five were built, and four served as commuters. Not as svelte as the Speedways, they combined the comforts of a houseboat with the speed of a commuter. The first of these, the 81′ × 14′6″ × 4′ *Nashira,* was built in 1924 for Richard F. Hoyt of New York. With an enclosed pilothouse forward followed by a large saloon, she had a good-sized afterdeck and cockpit along with three staterooms below and plenty of light and ventilation. *Nashira* was a comfortable vessel—and she was fast for such a large package. Powered by twin 500-hp Wright Typhoon V-12s, she stepped out at almost 30 mph. This was as good as many of the smaller and lighter express cruisers of the Jazz Age. Richard Hoyt's serious commuter was *Teaser,* a famous George Crouch design built by Nevins and powered by a single Wright Typhoon V-12 for better than 50 mph. The 39′10″ × 7′6″ *Teaser* beat the time of the Twentieth Century Limited between Albany and New York in 1925. *Teaser* was a bonitarian commuter although she was essentially a speedboat, an enlarged version of Caleb Bragg's famous Gold Cup racer *Baby Bootlegger.* The second Consolidated houseboat-cruiser was *Zinganee II,* built in 1925 for E. S. Moore of New York. She was powered by two 550-hp Typhoons and would run at more than 30 mph. Others were *Ardea* and *Kegonsa* in 1926, and *Pamnorm,* built for Norman B. Woolworth in 1930.

During the 1920s, Consolidated also built commuters to outside designs for their preferred clients. Favored were the John H. Wells renditions of larger commuters such as Gordon Hamersley's 75-foot *Cigarette* and the 80-foot *Lura M III* for W. A. Fisher of Detroit. In 1930, Consolidated built three outstanding Wells-designed commuters—the 75-foot *Cossack,* the 81-foot *Sazarac,* and the 75′6″ *Jem.* *Cossack,* built for George Moffett, was a familiar sight on Long Island Sound in the 1930s and 1940s. *Sazarac* blew up at her mooring when her fuel shut-off valves were left on after a run. *Jem,* now *Jessica,* the

73

most famous of the trio, is much admired by antique-boat enthusiasts, and appears at East Coast vintage-boat shows and the periodic gatherings of commuters. *Jem* was built for Jeremiah E. Milbank, hence the name, and Captain Raymond Thombs has been her devoted custodian since the end of World War II. Captain Thombs, along with *Jessica*'s latest owner, Ted Valpey, Jr., of New Hampshire, are responsible for *Jessica*'s extraordinary condition at over sixty years of age.

Jessica's history is of interest: From her original owner she passed into George Lauder's famous antique-boat collection. In 1987, upon George Lauder's death, the collection was given to Mystic Seaport Museum. When Ted Valpey purchased *Jessica* from Mystic Seaport, it was with the understanding that Captain Thombs would remain with her as long as he desired. Together they have logged many miles up and down the East Coast, attending both the 1989 and 1991 commuter gatherings. If there were a commuter-fleet leader it would have to be Captain Thombs at the helm of *Jessica*.

Consolidated built more commuters by far than any other firm, especially in the glory days between World War I and the deepening of the Depression in 1932–33. It is a tribute to the yard that so many of them have survived.

Another major builder of commuter yachts in the 1920s and 1930s was the Luders Marine Construction Company, founded by Alfred E. Luders, a graduate of the Webb Institute of Naval Architecture, in 1908. According to Weston Farmer, known to three generations of boatbuilders, Alfred E. began his career with Elco in New Jersey, and in 1907 had already designed an advanced step hydroplane. He set up for himself at East Port Chester, now known as Byram, Connecticut, on Long Island Sound, then moved to the west branch of Stamford harbor where he soon developed one of America's great yacht yards. By 1912 a stock 36-foot fast cruiser was being turned out, and at the beginning of World War I Luders Marine was designing and building fast military boats for owners interested in using their express cruisers for coastal defense and scouting. Out of this work, in 1916, came a 66-foot express/scout type that was "accepted by the United States

CIGARETTE

Another, later L. Gordon Hamersley commuter, this is the 75-foot Wells-designed, Nevins-built boat; similar to Cossack, Frolic II, *and* Jessica. *These commuters had splendid accommodations and were well liked by their owners. Of the five or so built,* Cigarette *and* Jessica *are still in use.*

LURA M III

A John Wells–designed Consolidated similiar to Cossack, Jessica, *and* Frolic II. *Most of these successful commuters were powered by large Winton twins. This Consolidated belonged to W. A. Fisher of the Detroit Yacht Club.*

SAZARAC

The first George Townsend Sazarac, she was built in 1923 by Great Lakes Boat Building in Milwaukee, Wisconsin and powered by Hall-Scott Invaders. Here she is in 1924 flying the owner's private signal and the burgee of the Indian Harbor Yacht Club (Greenwich, Connecticut).

JEM (JESSICA)

Except for a few minor details, this photograph could have been taken in the 1990s instead of the 1930s. Kept in top shape for forty-six years by Captain Raymond Thombs, the passage of the years and consistent use has not aged this Wells-designed Consolidated. In this photo she is shown early in her life at the Yale–Harvard boat races with Jeremiah Milbank's private signal flying and a light pearl-gray hull.

Navy Department as the best type of all designs submitted by the leading naval architects of the country," or so Luders advertising boasted at the time. This "best type" was a purposeful boat with a pronounced hard chine and mounting a 3-pound deck gun. Twin 400-hp V-12 Van Blerck engines delivered a top speed of 26 knots. There was a market for this type of boat during the war and shortly after. One of the most impressive was *Mystery*, designed by Tams, Lemoine and Crane and built by Luders for Ralph Pulitzer of New York, who offered her to the government for the exorbitant fee of one dollar a month. *Mystery* cost Pulitzer more than $30,000 in 1917 dollars. She was 71′3″ long with a beam of only 13′, and powered by two 400-hp Duesenberg 8-cylinder Patrol Model engines for a speed of 24 knots. After serving for two years she was returned to her owners in 1919 for civilian use, and the Pulitzer family used her at Joseph Pulitzer's summer home, commuting to Bar Harbor, and then at Ralph's home in Port Washington to run in and out of New York. Later use in the rum wars has been hinted at, but no records have been found to substantiate such a thing.

By the time *Mystery* came along, the Luders Marine Construction Company was one of the foremost eastern boatyards, turning out everything from Gold Cup raceboats to one-design sailboats and big cruising yachts, sail and power. The middle of the 1920s saw the beginnings of the Luders stock commuters when the good-looking 42-footers began to be built. These distinctive 30-mph mahogany cruisers had an enclosed deckhouse or "cab" amidships, with a low trunk cabin forward ending in a small forward cockpit. The Sterling Dolphin engines—earlier versions had a single power plant, later 42-foot Luders commuters had twins—lived under a somewhat narrow trunk cabin abaft the cab. This ended forward of a substantial after cockpit. According to Bill Luders, seven of these attractive boats were launched.

As a later result of Ralph Pulitzer's *Mystery* and the 66-foot scout type allegedly praised by the navy, a series of 70- to 75-foot commuters was developed, and these included the 72-foot *Applejack* in 1927 and the 72-foot *Geredna* in 1930. These were expanded, high-powered versions of the 42-footers—handsome, long, and low. Bill Luders took over design work from his father during the 1920s, designing many of the sailboats built by the yard, and the 70- to 75-foot commuters were enlarged in the late 1920s and early 1930s to produce such boats as *Catamount*, an 83-footer for Brad Ellsworth; *Sea Owl*, a 100-footer for Powel Crosley, Jr.; and *Robadore*, a 107-footer for Robert Law.

The name Luders ranks with Herreshoff, Consolidated, Lawley, and Purdy as one of the preeminent commuting-yacht builders of its day. Luders commuters and express cruisers were rakish, military-looking boats with distinct "streamlining" that began in the late twenties and became more pronounced in the thirties. The beautiful bow scrollwork on Luders commuters and express cruisers is seldom seen today—not many of these boats have survived.

The infield of the Indianapolis Motor Speedway, of all places, was the first boatyard of a third great 1920s commuter-building team—the Purdy brothers, Edward D. (Ned) and Gilbert (Gil) Purdy. The history of the Purdy Boat Company begins with Carl Graham Fisher— auto-industry pioneer, visionary and venture capitalist, real-estate developer, and lover of fast boats. Fisher started his business career at an early age, hawking candy and magazines on trains. He became a bicycle salesman and racer, setting a few records, and then began racing cars. He ran against the great, cigar-chomping Barney Old-field, among other dirt-track heroes. Oldfield never smoked, he just used the cigars to bite on as he manhandled the brutish cars of early motor racing. From these contests came Fisher's scheme for the greatest racetrack in the country—the Indianapolis Motor Speedway, built in 1909 with 3,200,000 paving bricks. Fisher made his first fortune with automobiles, having founded the Prest-O-Lite Company, maker of carbide headlights, which in the days before the all-electric car provided the only reliable light for night driving.

When he was forty years old he retired—but not for long. He took an interest in yachting, ballooning, promoting America's first long-distance highways, developing real estate in Montauk and Port Washington on Long Island, and—his biggest project—building a resort city on an island full of snakes and alligators in Florida. In 1912 Carl

CATAMOUNT

The 85-foot commuter by Luders Marine Construction built for Bradford Ellsworth. The sloping deckhouses and arched windows, typical of Luders designs, are noticeable. With cabins painted grayish-white and a black hull, she was a little different.

Fisher lent John Collins the money for the first bridge across Biscayne Bay from Miami to Miami Beach. It opened on May 22, 1913, with much fanfare, and Fisher began to develop a city on the other side. Another of his Florida ideas never got off the ground (or water). Fisher, Will Rogers, and Captain Charlie Thompson, the great Florida fishing guide, set up the Ocean Dairy Products Company to can sea-cow milk from the Florida manatee. To date no one has been found who has ever tasted the stuff.

While Fisher was promoting the 200 acres of sand and swamp he had acquired from John Collins, and perhaps milking manatees, he paid a call on Consolidated in New York to see about some yacht business. He was so impressed by the skills of two brothers, Ned and Gil Purdy, who worked in Consolidated's design department, that he hired them away and set them up with their own shop. The Purdy Boat Company built its first two boats, *Raven I* and *Raven II*, for Carl Fisher in 1916 in garages on the infield of the Indianapolis Speedway. The *Ravens* were express cruisers that served the U.S. Navy as patrol boats in World War I. In 1917 Fisher moved the Purdy Boat Company to Miami Beach, on a new street he named Purdy Avenue just across the Collins Bridge—now the Venetian Causeway. Here the first boat built for Fisher was called *Shadow III*, the first of a series of *Shadows* and *Ravens* that would compete in cruiser races from Miami to Key West and Miami to Havana in the late teens and early twenties. In 1917 the 51-foot *Raven III*, with 800 hp, won the inaugural Miami-to-Key-West Race at an average speed of 31.1 mph.

The boats built by the Purdys were fast, elegant commuters with high, sharp bows, and they were a whole new design development. While Bill Hand, John Hacker, Napoleon Lisee, Chris Smith, and others were developing a hard-chine, V-bottom type of planing hull, the Purdys favored a sharp forward section, flared out at the cap rails and with a nice curve to the stem below the waterline, and with a bottom that had rounded chine lines. A fair amount of tumble home, or inward slant, at the top of the rounded transom was a Purdy trademark, and a sweeping curve of sheerline was another distinctive feature of these beautiful boats. A handsome, bronze-cast, transom-hung, single rudder finished off the exercise. While not as fast as the Gar Wood and Chris Smith boats in the Florida express-cruiser races, Purdy boats more than held their own when the seas picked up and the going got rougher. The Purdys built cruisers, racing boats, even a few sailboats on Purdy Avenue, but the Florida summers were too hot for them and Fisher moved the Purdy Boat Company to Trenton, Michigan, in 1921. In Michigan they turned out *Shadow F* for Fisher, a slim 72′ × 14′ commuter that later became a much-admired commuting yacht on Long Island Sound under the ownership of Herbert Pratt as *Whisper*. In Michigan the Purdys also built the famous Biscayne Babies—18-foot one-design raceboats for Fisher's Florida clients, all powered by 100-hp Scripps engines for speeds to 35 mph. One of these went to England and passed into the hands of an Aircraftsman who called himself T. E. Shaw. The Aircraftsman—who loved fast boats, fast motorcycles, and fast camels—had been known as Lawrence of Arabia a decade before. Lawrence/Shaw took over this boat in 1929 and put her in prime condition, learning about fast boats and their engines in the process, and with the great British powerboat designer Hubert Scott-Paine he helped to develop Royal Air Force rescue boats in 1930 and 1931. The Purdy brothers' little 18-footer must have been inspiration for this work.

In 1925 the Purdys moved again—this time to Port Washington on Manhasset Bay—by the midtwenties a principal port for Long Island commuters. Here the well-known commuters *Rascal, Annabar, Miss Larchmont IV, Shadow-Fay, Carryall,* and the last impressive Purdy commuter, *Aphrodite,* were built. Carl Fisher, who had seen the end of his and everyone else's Florida land boom, and was beginning to feel the effects of the Depression by the early 1930s, gave the entire operation—land, buildings, and equipment—to Ned and Gil Purdy. In 1932 the Bank of North Hempstead failed, nearly wiping out the Purdys. All their funds were in that bank. But the bank, being service-oriented, came through and paid Ned and Gil a generous 10 cents on the dollar. This catastrophe hastened Ned's death in 1933. During World War II the Purdy Boat Company became a defense contractor, building eighty-eight boats for the navy. Like many anoth-

WHISPER
This lovely Purdy design was built for Carl Fisher as Shadow F. Pictured in 1923 when owned by Edward S. Moore of Roslyn, Long Island, she was 72 feet and powered by two magnificent V-12 Allison engines (only eight built, and $22,500 each in 1922). Her large single, transom-hung, Purdy rudder is noticeable.

er great yacht-building enterprise of the first four decades of this century, this one did not long survive in the new postwar world of small boats, stock boats, and hardly any yacht commuting. By 1950 what had been the Purdy Boat Company was a service-and-repair yard.

A few express-yacht builders from across the Atlantic entered the growing market for commuters during the twenties. Lürssen of Germany built *Charming Polly* for Colonel H. H. Rogers of New York City in 1926. *Charming Polly* was 76′ with 13′6″ beam and powered by two beautifully made V-12 Maybach Zeppelin gasoline engines for a guaranteed cruising speed of 34 mph. In the City Island boatyards of the time, the painters and yard hands would put down their tools and turn their eyes to Long Island Sound as *Charming Polly* roared past with the sound and fury of the same engines that powered the great German dirigibles. In 1927 the impressive 73-foot *Oheka II* was built by Lürssen for the Metropolitan Opera Company's Otto Kahn. She

was powered by three V-12 Maybach Zeppelins. In Sweden, the Forslund brothers and Knud Reimers built a few commuters for U.S. clients.

In England, the renowned Camper and Nicholson shipyard developed a commuter type that was largely used as a tender for "Big Class" yachts during their final glorious decade of racing—the Gelyce Class of 50′ × 8′ tender-commuters. Six of these slender, elegant boats were built in the late twenties and early thirties, and three of them are still around, one in the United States. In 1988 that intrepid antique-boat collector, Jim Lewis of Clayton, New York, acquired the impeccably restored *Mavourneen* from Peter Freebody and had her shipped to these shores. *Mavourneen* is a sedan type with long varnished foredeck, fore and aft cockpits, and a day cabin in between. The foredeck is about a third of the length of the boat and houses the 320-hp Chevrolet/Pleasurecraft V8 under almost flush hatches. The deep forward cockpit with a helm station begins almost amidships. Aft is the pleasant sedan cabin with two narrow bunk-settees and an enclosed head. In the stern is the aft cockpit.

Mavourneen was in the process of restoration for more than three years in the famous Peter Freebody boatyard at Hurley on the Thames, England's premier restoration shop. Reposing in an ancient back shed when I last visited Freebody's a few years ago was *Gelyce* herself, awaiting rebuilding for British yachtsman and America's Cup challenger Peter de Savary. The third survivor, *Herring Gull,* is owned by Peter Freebody himself. During my visit Peter could not say what her disposition would be, as scattered about the premises were other interesting boats in various stages of repair and disrepair, along with two serious classic autos—a Bugatti and a Lagonda.

At the Antique and Classic Boat Society show at the Deering estate in Miami in 1988, *Mavourneen* made her American debut. After the show was over, Jim Lewis's son, Larry, his wife, Patti, and the author took *Mavourneen* up Biscayne Bay in 3- to 4-foot seas on a blustery morning. She was doing about 25 knots knifing through the chop, and being long and narrow the ride was surprisingly smooth. As we pulled up on a 52-foot Hatteras running at flank speed and

83

sliced through her sizeable wake, everyone aboard the Hatteras moved to the port rail with cameras clicking and mouths open in disbelief as we flashed by. *Mavourneen* gets attention wherever she goes.

As a day boat for gentlemen and ladies watching the great yacht races of the thirties in England, *Mavourneen* may be stretching the definition of commuter a bit, but she is a wonderful example of the British commuter-tenders built in the glory days of yachting.

Between the two world wars, the up-to-date yacht-design firms that specialized in commuters in the United States favored a patrol-boat type along the lines of those developed by A. Loring Swasey and George Crouch, professor of mathematics at the renowned Webb Institute of Naval Architecture. Many of these interesting, no-nonsense types were from the boards of Tams, Lemoine and Crane, founded by James Frederic Tams in the 1890s. Tams, Lemoine and Crane had designed Ralph Pulitzer's influential 71-foot *Mystery* during World War I, and in the first half of the twenties the firm's designs for express yachts and commuters included the 61-foot *Oheka*, built by Nevins in 1925 for Otto Kahn. In 1926 the partnership designed the

84

58-foot *Greyhound,* built by Wood and McClure for Edsel Ford, and the 60-foot *Brook II,* built by Julius Peterson for Percy Pyne II, who commuted 60 miles a day to and from his Wall Street offices. On the weekends she logged several hundred miles of cruising. *Brook II* had twin Sterlings, not as much power as Edsel Ford's *Greyhound,* which suited her name with two Liberty V-12s pushing her to 33 mph.

In 1927, Tams, Lemoine and Crane became Tams and King with Albert (Ab) Crouch, George's brother, becoming secretary after Fred Chase had left. Ab Crouch designed *Whim III* for banker Harrison Williams while he was with Tams and King—a famous twenties commuter advertised as offering "railroad speed on the water." *Whim III* was a 56-foot single-step hydroplane with twin V-12 Wright Typhoon engines of 650 hp each, a flyer built by Consolidated in 1928 that flew on her trial runs at 52 mph. The Wright Typhoon engines that were rated for 500 hp in 1925 had been boosted to 150 more horses by 1928. Other Tams and King designs of the midtwenties were *Phantom,* a 66-footer built for Ralph Pulitzer in 1927 by the Nevins yard, and *Lotty K,* a 49-footer built by Peterson for Adolph Zukor, the motion-picture

MAVOURNEEN
One of the three J-Boat Tenders built by the renowned English yard of Camper & Nicholsons in 1930. She is a long, smooth 50' x 50' day commuter, currently used by the Lewis family at their home in the Thousand Lakes, but seen here running down Biscayne Bay in the 1990s.

magnate. With twin V-12 Typhoons, *Phantom* did 45 mph. Great care had been taken by the designers of *Whim III* and *Phantom* so that the forward ends of the deck structures acted as wind deflectors. As for *Lotty K,* in 1927 she was said to be the Hudson River's fastest commuter. With twin V-12 Packards giving her better than 50 mph, she must have been.

A similar boat to *Whim* and *Phantom* was *Rascal II.* Not to be outdone by a banker and a newspaper publisher, the Wright-Martin Corporation's Caleb Bragg—engine-builder, aviator, auto racer, and speedboat competitor—had the Purdy brothers build him the flashing *Rascal* in 1929. With twin V-12 Packards driving her step-bottomed hull at 55-plus mph, *Rascal II* was an ultra-commuter and probably the fastest on Long Island Sound at the end of the decade. A society magazine reported that after a particularly vibrating run across the Sound one of Caleb's guests on board suffered a bit of rearrangement of her bridgework. A gentleman, Caleb ran the boat back to the Purdys, whereupon she was hauled and the step was removed from her bottom. The result was a somewhat slower but more civilized ride for this awesome 50-foot, 50-knot flyer.

Other outstanding commuter designers of the Jazz Age were John H. Wells, Walter McInnis, and John Hacker. Wells designed a dozen great commuters, many of them built by Consolidated. In 1928 his design firm produced Gordon Hamersley's last *Cigarette,* a $75' \times 12'11' \times 4'$ blade powered by two 6-cylinder Winton engines for close to 30 mph. And a contemporary testament to his sleek, conservative design style is *Jessica*—along with the Purdys' *Aphrodite* the biggest and most spectacular of today's restored commuters. Wells designed two twenties commuters for Walter Chrysler: the 70-foot *Frolic II* built by Lawley, successor to a 62-foot Consolidated, and the 75-foot *Frolic III* built by Mathis. Walter McInnis, who apprenticed at Lawley's and had many of the yachts he designed built there, was also famous in the 1920s for designing rumrunners, which appeared on his drawings and contracts as "cargo boats." He was also renowned for businesslike commercial and government vessels, and many of his commuters had a distinctive, exalted-workboat look to

PHANTOM

The distinctive patrol-boat type designed for Ralph Pulitzer to commute from his home in Port Washington, Long Island, to the NYYC station at 23rd Street. This 45-mph commuter was from the boards of Tams and King, built by the Nevins yard. Powered by twin V-12 Wright Typhoons, she is flying the owner's private signal and the burgee of the Larchmont Yacht Club. Note the venturi-effect windshield.

WHIM III

The very fast Tams-and-King-designed commuter built by Consolidated for Harrison Williams of New York. Originally she had step-bottom, and was capable of over 50 mph. The step was later removed but she still moved along at a great rate with her twin V-12 Wright Typhoons.

LOTTY K

An unusual Tams design built for the film mogul, Adolph Zukor. With her twin V-12 Packards she was thought by some to be the fastest commuter on the Hudson. The crew controlled boat from the forward cockpit which could have been rough in dusty conditions. The Packards were directly aft.

RASCAL

One of the fastest commuters on Long Island Sound. With her original step-bottom she achieved over 50 mph. The step was later removed as concession to guests' comfort but she was still fast. Designed and built by Purdy brothers for sportsman Caleb Bragg and powered by Packards, she was later used as a rumrunner.

them. The outstanding example is *Marlin,* designed for Edsel Ford in
1930, owned for a time by the Kennedy family, and another survivor
now serving new owners on Long Island. John Hacker, legendary
designer of raceboats and mahogany speedboats, produced a number
of express yachts and commuters in the 1920s and 1930s, the largest an 85-footer, *Rosewill,* built in 1926 by Defoe Boat Works for W.
C. Rand. Hacker was one of the few commuter designers with a
worldwide reputation and clientele—in 1930 he designed a 40-foot
limousine-style commuter for the king of Siam that was said to be
capable of 60 mph.

Hacker's commuter for the king, if it did travel a mile-a-minute,
would have been the fastest boat of the golden age of yacht commuting between World War I and the depths of the Depression. But
a series of "stock" 50-foot commuters nearly as fast came along in the
mid-1920s as a result of the racing, engine-building and boatbuilding
enterprises of Gar Wood.

Garfield Arthur Wood, one of thirteen brothers and sisters, was
born in 1880 on a farm in Iowa and named after two presidents. His
Gar Wood boats were considered the Buicks of Jazz Age mahogany
runabouts, with Chris-Craft products being the Chevrolets and John
Hacker's stock speedboats being the Cadillacs. And the 50-foot commuters Gar Wood produced in the 1920s were something like Ferraris.
They even had V-12 engines.

Gar Wood's first race was in his father's steam ferryboat against a
rival ferry considered the fastest on Lake Osakis in Minnesota. In the
best Mississippi River steamboat tradition, Gar and his father dis-
membered most of the wooden chairs and tables and fed the pieces
into the firebox, enabling their *Manitoba* to steam to a glorious finish. Evidently young Gar never forgot this. By the age of thirteen Gar
Wood was running the first gasoline-powered launch around Duluth.
As word of his skills with boats and gas engines got around, Gar was
asked to build other fast little boats (about 15 mph), and by 1911, mod-
erately backed by some of the locals, he was racing speedboats on the
Midwest circuit with great success.

Gar Wood was yet another Midwest farm boy with a very inven-

FROLIC II

Walter P. Chrysler's first John Wells–designed, 70-foot, Lawley-built commuter. The reason for the large foredeck covering is unknown. This was an enduring John Wells design very similiar to his Cigarette, Jessica, *and* Frolic III.

FROLIC III

The third of Walter P. Chrysler's Wells-designed commuters. This one, built by Mathis Yacht of Camden, New Jersey, is flying the New York Yacht Club burgee. Note the John Wells bow scrollwork.

tive mind, and in 1912 he built a hydraulic device to raise the beds of trucks, using junkyard parts and gears he cut in his backyard machine shop. This was the beginning of the Wood Hydraulic Hoist and Body Company, and the firm soon provided every truck builder in the country with something new—the dump truck. It also provided Gar Wood the money to play with fast boats for the rest of his life.

In 1914 Gar Wood, with his family and business, moved to Detroit where he met Chris Smith, the patriarch of what would become Chris-Craft. Knowing a good thing when he saw it, he bought into the Chris Smith and Sons boatbuilding operation. By 1917 the Wood family and the Smith family were competing in the prestigious Gold Cup races, which Jay Smith and Gar Wood won that year in *Miss Detroit III.* Gar Wood went on to dominate the Gold Cup for the next four years, won Britain's Harmsworth Trophy in 1920, and set an extraordinary World Water Speed Record of 77.89 mph in 1920 aboard *Miss America I,* a 26-foot hull built by Chris Smith and pushed by two Liberty V-12 engines.

After World War I, the availability of surplus aircraft power plants at bargain prices was an opportunity to be seized. Gar Wood established the Detroit Marine Aero Engine Company, purchasing Beardmore, Benz, F.I.A.T., Liberty, and Mercedes engines along with quantities of spare parts, and in 1920 he and his team of designers and boatbuilders developed a 50-foot express yacht powered by twin Gar Wood Liberties. With this boat, *Gar Jr. II,* he set a Miami-to-Palm-Beach cruiser record early in 1921. A week later he won a Miami-to-Key-West cruiser race at an average of 38 mph. Two months later Gar and Charles F. Chapman, editor of *Motor Boating,* took this proto-commuter offshore to race the Havana Special, the crack train of the Atlantic Coast Line between Miami and New York. Running for 1,260 miles in the bumpy Atlantic, with five fuel stops (1,800 gallons), *Gar Jr. II* took 47 hours and 23 minutes to beat the time of the express train by 21 minutes. This must have been the longest and most-publicized commuter run in history.

Between 1923 and 1928 a number, perhaps as many as ten, of these mega-speedboats were built as commuters; they were 50 feet long with

ROSEWILL

An impressive Hacker and Fermann–designed commuter, built by Defoe Boat and Motor of Bay City, Michigan, for the Rand family of Detroit in 1926. Her formidable bridge and control station cannot be seen. Powered by twin V-12 Packards, she was another fast John Hacker commuter, shown here flying owners' private signal and Detroit Yacht Club burgee.

Rosewill's *well-laid-out flying bridge of the late 1920s. John Hacker's design work is evident in this 1927 photograph. Nothing is left out—horns, lights, controls, etc.*

Rosewill's *forward deckhouse and second helm station The radio to port was state of the art at the time.*

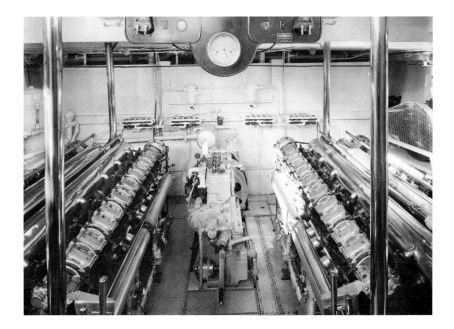

Looking forward in Rosewill's *engine room at the unusually clean Liberty V-12 conversions by Packard. An atlas generator is in the center. Note the elaborate gasoline fuel-filtering system on the forward gas tank.*

10′3″ beam, and they came with two Gar Wood Liberties of 450 hp each. They were usually repowered later because of corrosion problems that accompanied both Liberty and Hispano-Suiza engines in marine use. Two of the most famous of these commuters were Marshall Field's *Corisande* and *Tamarack V* for Dr. H. N. Torrey of Detroit.

Following the time-honored design and engineering axiom that more speed requires bigger engines and bigger engines require a larger boat, Gar Wood developed a 70-foot commuter type with an 11′6″ beam in 1923, and powered the boat with no fewer than four Liberty engines. His *Gar Sr.* was soon sold to Gordon Hamersley—financier, speedboat racer, and Long Island sportsman and patrician—who renamed her *Cigarette,* the same name he had given a previous commuter designed by William Hand (and a name borrowed from the 1905 steam commuter built by the Lawley yard for William H. Ames). The new owner added a fifth Gar Wood–prepared Liberty engine to the boat for a total of 2,250 hp. As the fastest of Hamersley's several *Cigarettes,* this impressive machine would roar down the East River at full gallop, delivering her owner to Wall Street and occasionally stopping traffic on the East River Drive. Gar Wood must have built her very well, as the hull was still afloat in Mt. Clemens, Michigan, in 1990, although much altered as a liveaboard.

One of the myths surrounding this boat is that she became a rum-runner. In the early twenties there was a Brooklyn rumrunner called *Cigarette,* owned by a gangster named Valentine Higgins and described by the Coast Guard as "a chronic offender" when she was chased but not caught on Valentine's Day (oddly enough) in 1924. The 70-foot Gar Wood *Cigarette* was nearly new in early 1924 and still owned by Gordon Hamersley of Wall Street and Long Island. They were not the same boat. Nevertheless, a few fast commuters and express yachts did become rumboats, notably *Sovereign* (later *Vereign*)—Matthew Borden's *Little Sovereign* of 1904, and rumboats named *Whispering Winds* and *Atalanta*—both with a definite commuter look about them.

Gar Wood's boatbuilding empire produced elite speedboats during the 1920s and 1930s, and Gar Wood Boats advertised heavily in the

GAR SR.

Built as Cigarette *for Gordon Hamersley and later owned by Gar Wood, she is shown here in 1926 all dressed out, alongside a Consolidated Speedway series commuter. An enclosed bridge has been added and the forward-deck couch has been removed, but she was still powered by five Libertys.*

yachting and business magazines of the time. When the Depression was hitting bottom in 1934, the company was offering a line of thirty-six models that included commuters. The old advertising slogan of "the Aristocrat of Motor Boats" became in the 1930s "the Greatest Name in Motorboating." Gar Wood Boats survived until 1948, building landing and assault craft for the government during World War II. The last commuter offered was in 1941. While never achieving the volume production of commuters as did Chris-Craft in the late 1920s and early 1930s, the company built some of the fastest commuters of the Jazz Age, and the name Gar Wood—holder of the World Water Speed Record for most of the years from 1920 to 1933—had cachet.

Chris-Craft, always astute about finding markets for its boats or, better yet, creating stock boats for an existing market, had been mass-producing mahogany speedboats at the low end of the price range since 1922. Chris Smith and his sons created the Ford Motor Company of the boating world, and they were successful enough by 1927 to begin building their own engines and to expand the product line from runabouts to cruisers. The first Chris-Craft engines were a 200-hp V8 and a 150-hp six, and the first cruisers were commuters. In 1928 they brought what they called a 30-foot Custom Commuter to the New York Motor Boat Show. Not a runabout conversion, this boat was an all-new sedan type with a single 200-hp Chris-Craft V8, a fast day boat that could sleep two during a cruise on seat/berths aft of the helmsman in the forward cabin. The head was located in a curious open position in a cockpit just forward of the engine compartment. The 30-foot Custom Commuter, definitely a middle-class addition to the commuter fleet of the twenties, was priced with full equipment at $9,750. This boat was a unique addition to the Chris-Craft line, and ten of these Model 11s were built in 1928. Chris-Craft was onto something in the peak years of yacht commuting, and with much fanfare the revolutionary 38-foot Commuting Cruiser came out in November of 1928. This was—and still is—one of the company's great boats. Fully equipped even down to a Rudy Vallee–style megaphone, and powered by Chris-Craft's own V8 engine, the price was $15,000.

The Chris-Craft 30- and 38-foot boats were the first production-built commuters to hit the market, and the 38-foot Model 122 was a huge success. Until the Depression flattened the boating business, sixty-five of these elegant 30-mph boats were delivered through 1931. The author's Commuter Register shows that sixteen Chris-Craft 38-foot commuters are in use or being restored, among them *Excalibur, Friendship, Linda Mar, Red Witch, Simokon,* and *Tradition.* Having been through a bad storm aboard Mike Matheson's *Tradition* on Long Island Sound, I can testify that these enlarged Chris-Craft runabouts are not bad sea boats. But like Captain Voss, I can say that *Tradition* "iss strong but vet." Four of these boats joined the 1991 Commuter Rendezvous—*Fire One, Red Witch, Sue Lyn Cyn,* and *Tradition.* A short commuter race was run among the 38-footers at the end of the rendezvous under the direction of Bob MacKay. The results are still unfathomable.

In the ominous year of 1929, Chris-Craft introduced two more stock commuters—the 34-foot Model 121 Custom Commuter and the Model 123 48-foot Commuting Yacht. The 34-footer, powered by twin 225-hp Chris-Craft V8s for 40 mph, was priced at $15,000. The 48-footer, powered by two of the same engines for 30 mph, was $35,000. The production run for these boats was short-lived; four of the 34-footers and five of the 48s were built. But with the company suffering a $200,000-plus loss at the end of 1931, Chris-Craft built no more commuters and switched strategy to the more marketable utility-boat line with prices that started at $695. The company survived the Depression building smaller boats than the commuters and drastically reducing the product line—only four models in the worst year, 1933—then resumed cruiser construction in 1937 with a fleet of ninety-five models, forty-two of them cruising boats. None of these new cruisers were commuters. When the Great Depression ended is a matter for dispute; but it appears to have ended for Chris-Craft in 1937, and the company sailed profitably through the war years with government contracts and became, in the 1950s, the world's largest producer of pleasure boats. Chris-Craft, a household word since the early 1920s, is one of the few pre-Depression boatbuilders still around. Another one is Huckins.

CHRIS-CRAFT

The fully found, completely equipped 38-foot Chris-Craft commuter as shown at the 1929 Motor Boat Show at Grand Central Palace in New York City. The navy top is carried in its closed position. A lot of boat for only fifteen grand! Right: a typical interior of a boat in the 34-foot range.

The opening of the 24th-annual Motor Boat Show at the Grand Central Palace, New York City, in the last week of January was the first important yachting event in 1929. There were three things I was looking forward to in those days—getting the all-important driver's license, the last day of school, and the New York Boat Show. By the late 1920s the show took up three floors of the many-pillared Grand Central Palace, with Port Elco right next door. It was at the 1929 show that Frank Pembroke Huckins displayed the wares of the Huckins Yacht Corporation, which he had formed the previous year. Using a small booth at the show, along with some persuasive advertising copy, six orders were taken for Huckins's 45-foot twin-screw cruiser-commuters. These boats were powered by two 6-cylinder 225-hp Kermath Sea Wolfs, engines that delivered 20 knots. They were completely equipped down to linens, cookware, and Ovington's flag-marked china for the astonishing price of $19,000 afloat at the plant in Jacksonville. This was a successful boat for the small yard on the Ortega River. Along with a smaller and less-expensive model, it got Huck and the yard through the worst of the Depression years.

Frank Huckins was an opinionated, sometimes irritating, genius with interesting and controversial ideas when it came to boats. His treatise on hull design, "The Quadraconic Hull," published by *Motor Boating* in 1952, brings out most of his firm convictions in a fairly understandable manner, although the definition of the quadraconic hull is never fully addressed. Huckins's deliberately lightweight yachts had a warped-plane, V-bottomed, fully planing hull that incorporated a laminated keel and stem. At first a double-diagonal skin of thin mahogany covered the light framework, and later this was sheathed in fiberglass. Whether Huckins would have gone along with fiberglass sheathing for the boats he called Fairform Flyers is a moot question; it added weight, and weight was one of his obsessions. Huckins died in 1951, and the company carried on its tradition of light, fast, businesslike boats and adopted new techniques and materials. Since 1977 Airex, a rigid PVC closed-cell foam, has been the core material in the construction of Huckins yachts. Huckins's boats were big, fast, somewhat stark cruisers and motor yachts with transom-hung rudders. Below the water the keel was minimal, and when up on top they skidded in fast turns. As a testimony to the durability of a Huckins, of the 430-odd boats built since 1929 more than 300 are still in commission.

Frank Huckins was a vivid and convincing copywriter of the Huckins ads that always appeared on the first page of every issue of *Motor Boating*—so much so that I broke down a few years ago, after avidly reading Huckins's ads for decades, and mortgaged the farm to purchase a Fairform Flyer built in 1962. We lived aboard this 53-foot Offshore Model for two and a half years in Florida, and *Quicksilver* was all she was supposed to be and then some. With the little signal mast down, we squeezed her under some mighty low bridges and also left behind some impressive sportfishermen when running outside.

Our *Quicksilver* had been built for a Florida sportsman who used her for big-game fishing and also commuted in her from a home in Pompano Beach to offices in Miami. She was a 1960s example of what Frank Huckins had in mind when he came to the New York Motor Boat Show in 1929. His early Fairform Flyers were intended as commuters, and at least one of the six 45-footers he sold in New York in 1929 served as a commuter.

The same year that Huckins began building and promoting fast yachts for cruising and commuting, a Michigan builder moved into a market that was definitely expanding in the late twenties. One of the largest builders of big speedboats and limousine-style commuters in the 1920s and 1930s was the Robinson Marine Construction Company, started in the mid-1920s at Benton Harbor, Michigan, about two hours out of Chicago. Robinson began concentrating on commuters in 1928 with their Seagull line, and their boats represented a new type that came along in the late twenties from several builders—a long, low, twin-screw speedboat with chauffeur's cockpit forward and a posh day cabin amidships. Although similar boats were built by Chris-Craft, Gar Wood, Dodge, and Hacker, they were a Robinson specialty.

By 1931 Robinson Marine offered as many as eight different commuter models. One of the most successful was the Seagull Sedan

Commuter, a well-built 39′ × 8′7″ mahogany hull with either one or two Kermath or Hall-Scott engines for power. With a cruising range of approximately 200 miles at 30 mph, this was a fast, elegant, reliable boat sold to commuting yachtsmen not only on the Great Lakes but on the East Coast as well. Very much on-the-water limousines, these boats were controlled from the forward cockpit and featured a leatherette-covered sedan top over a luxuriously appointed saloon with enclosed head. Aft was a roomy rear cockpit. The handsome Robinson Seagulls were designed by Walter Leveau, who also designed mahogany runabouts and sedans for the Horace E. Dodge Boat and Plane Corporation. Leveau designed Horace's Gold Cup boats *Delphine IV* and *Delphine VI.*

By the early 1930s, Robinson ads in *Rudder, Yachting,* and *Motor Boat* were proclaiming "Robinson Marine Construction Company— The Largest Builders of Speed Cruisers and Commuters." The firm considered its plant facilities and skilled personnel second to none, and so apparently did enough customers to keep Seagull fast cruisers and commuters abuilding through the hard times of the 1930s. These boats were luxury items—but like Cadillac, Packard, and Lincoln automobiles in the 1930s, their style and expensive substance may have been an advantage. Like the custom-bodied cars and some other products for the rich that came along during the Depression, they found a market among people who not only hadn't lost their money but were eager to spend it.

Robinson survived the Depression and even flourished, building a wide range of cruisers and commuters from 30 to 65 feet. The firm secured a few commitments from the government during World War II, and these contracts kept Robinson in business. But Robinson, like many other luxury boatbuilders, found the postwar world a different place. The glory days of the late twenties and even the thirties were gone forever, and the company had its last model year in 1948, the same year that saw Gar Wood Boats close its doors. A few of these fine commuters survive, and a few more are in the process of restoration now that old boats are considered valuable again—especially old boats with the style and performance of these marine limousines.

FOTO

Morris Rosenfeld's specially built photo boat, designed by Fred Lord. Many of the photographs in this book were taken aboard this boat, built by the Kanno Brothers on City Island, New York City. An exact restoration by Ed Cutts of Oxford, Maryland was undertaken a few years ago. She is shown here, around 1930, flying the flag of the Regatta Circuit Riders Club from the bow staff.

DORICA

A German boat from Lürssen with twin V-12 Maybach engines, shown here commuting from Rye to New York City in the 1930s with her owner, Charles Edge, aboard.

APHRODITE

The first Aphrodite commuter at speed off New London, Connecticut. The elaborate Albany Boat Works scroll shows on her starboard bow. She is flying the Whitney Greentree pennant and the New York Yacht Club burgee. Note the lovely curved glass forward windows of the deckhouse.

APHRODITE

The Whitney commuter is on its way to the Harvard–Yale boat races with a boatload of spectators. Her graceful and distinctive stern treatment was the model for the sterns of both Aphrodite III and Saga.

ARGO

A straightforward John Wells–designed commuter built by F. S. Nock in East Greenwich, Rhode Island. The New York Yacht Club burgee and the owner's signal are flying. A large forward cockpit can accommodate ten to twelve guests.

ARGO

The engine room of the 60-footer. The Sterling Dolphins are a matched pair of 2,300 pound, 290 hp sixes. Photograph taken in summer of 1926.

TAMARACK V

One of three or four of the 50-foot Gar Wood commuters built in the late 1920s. Powered by twin Gar Wood Libertys, they were quite fast as long as they were used in fresh water. She is flying the owner's signal and the Detroit Yacht Club burgee.

STROLLER

A distinctive smaller Herreshoff commuter built in 1929, for C. D. Rafferty of New York. Featuring a large forward and aft cockpit, she was mostly a day commuter, powered by twin Sterlings.

SHUTTLE

One of the lesser-known of the Morgan commuters. Built in 1928, by the Herreshoff Manufacturing Company of Bristol, Rhode Island, for Junius S. Morgan, she was used to go back and forth from Corsair, among other duties. Flying the Commodore's flag and the New York Yacht Club burgee.

UANI

A nice close-up of the popular Luders 42-foot commuter. This is possibly a publicity shot done by Rosenfeld in 1927. Unfortunately none of these good-looking boats have survived.

SEA HORSE

Designed and built by the Purdy Boat Company in 1921, in Trenton, Michigan, for James Allison, this graceful 80-foot commuter was powered by twin V-12 Allison gas engines costing $22,000 each in 1921. She is showing the burgee of the Detroit Yacht Club. Below: The smooth Purdy shown at the Detroit powerboat races of 1921. Purdy commuters had a graceful sheer and at times a large transom-hung rudder which can be seen. She was used for many years in the Great Lakes and Florida.

ROBMAR II

A straightforward Walter McInnis design, built by American Car and Foundry (acf) in Wilmington, Delaware for Mortimer Loewi. Shown in May of 1928, she was 45 feet, and powered by twin Hall-Scott Invaders.

SEA SCAMP

A 42-foot commuter designed by F.D. Lawley and built for Charles N. Edge by George Lawley and Son, of Neponset, Massachusetts. She is shown running along on the Hudson, flying the burgee of the Naskeag Yacht Club of Brooklin, Maine.

RICHELIEU

A fine-looking 80-foot Wells-Consolidated, commuter with a very graceful sheer built for the Reynolds family. Similiar in some ways to the Speedway series. She is shown in 1929, flying her owner's private signal and the Montauk Yacht Club burgee.

PHANTOM II

Built by Consolidated from a Tams and King design—much like Rascal, Vampire, *and* Whim—Phantom II *is strictly a day-boat commuter designed for high speed. She is flying owner's signals and the burgee of the Corinthian Yacht Club of Philadelphia.*

MAXINE

The Tex Rickart, John Wells-designed Lawley-built commuter running on Long Island Sound. The three forward bows are for a covered-wagon type canvas over the front cockpit. She is flying the burgee of the Larchmont Yacht Club.

MARIANNE (SHADOW III)

Originally one of the Purdy brothers' Shadows owned by Carl G. Fisher, was built in 1917. She is pictured celebrating the 4th of July in 1927. It could be Carl Fisher seated with cigar in forward cockpit.

MAROLD

This striking high-speed craft was built in 1914, by the venerable Matthews Boat Company of Ohio, one of the only commuters built by this large operation. Designed by John Wells, she originally sported a forward deck gun, as did many of the scout-patrol boats commissioned by private owners in World War I. Shown in 1927 off New London, Connecticut. The searchlight looks as if it could have melted anything in front of it when lit.

LITTLE VIKING

One of the numerous variations of Consolidated commuters. This one, a 70-footer, was built in 1927 for George F. Baker, Jr, of New York primarily as a day boat. The large aft cockpit is noticeable in this shot.

HIAWATHA

A 1924, 85-foot Consolidated for J. B. Ford of Detroit, running at about 20 knots. The stack was for decoration only. She was Consolidated Speedway powered.

IOTA

Built for Howard Ingersol in 1920 by Consolidated and originally named Lone Star *by same owner. Her first engines were Wright-Hissos, but later she was twin Speedway powered and her bus-type helm at first had no windshield.*

HELENA

A well-appointed Consolidated commuter built for C. E. F. McCann of New York in 1928. She was powered by twin Consolidated Speedway gasoline engines.

HARMATTAN

A German-built commuter designed by F. P. Humphreys for James Ottley of Glen Cove, Long Island, in 1928. She is 49 feet and looks larger.

116

BAMBALINA III
Luders Hull #337, built for Theodore Pratt. The Luders sloping cabins are noticeable. The forward cockpit is covered over in the dusty weather.

ALLEZ
One of the 48-foot Chris Crafts running on the Intracoastal Waterway in Palm Beach, Florida. In the background is the Palm Beach Biltmore Hotel and the Brazilian Docks. Allez is flying the Cleveland Yacht Club burgee from the bow staff.

CORISANDE

The 50-foot commuter by Gar Wood was built for Marshall Field. Her hull was constructed by Nevins at City Island. Well-known Captain John Stafford ran Field's boat for many years; he is at helm. She was powered by twin Libertys, then later by Wright Typhoon V-12s.

VANSANTA

A 92-foot commuter by Consolidated produced for George Pynchon of Greenwich, Connecticut, in 1926. Powered by the usual Consolidated Speedways, she is shown flying the owner's private signal and the NYYC burgee.

SAZARAC

The first of George Townsend's Sazaracs, built in 1923 by Great Lakes Boat Building in Milwaukee, Wisconsin. Powered by Hall-Scott Invaders, she is shown here in 1924 flying the owner's private signal and the burgee of the Indian Harbor Yacht Club (Greenwich, Connecticut).

TARA

A roomy commuter produced by the Herreshoff Company in 1920 for the avid yachtsman H. L. Maxwell of New York. At the same time he also owned Ballymena, *a 60-foot Consolidated, and* Banshee, *another Herreshoff of 59 feet.* Tara *is shown in the summer of 1927.*

TARA

The well-known commuter idling along on the Connecticut River in 1930. Now owned by E. Townsend Irving of New York, the comfortable raised-deck vessel is powered by twin Speedways.

Chapter Four

Carrying On Bravely

DESPITE INSOLVENT STOCK SPECULATORS JUMPING OUT OF WINDOWS and the beginnings of layoffs in manufacturing plants, nobody in 1930 thought what was then described as "the economic downturn" would last very long. The twenties had been such an exciting, bountiful time—with the rich getting richer and the poor getting enough to eat—that what we now know as the Great Depression seemed inconceivable. It remained inconceivable—or at least avoidable—for some. One of the remarkable things about the 1930s is how many exquisite services and products for the rich came to full flower in a time of economic distress—custom-bodied automobiles, luxury liners for extravagant travel to Europe, nightclubs and great hotels full of white-tie and silk-gown celebrants very much like Fred Astaire and Ginger Rogers on the screen, the J-Boats and Big Class yachts of international sailing, and the greatest of the commuters.

Yacht commuting reached a peak in the season of 1930, with at least a hundred of the flyers making daily trips to Manhattan. It had been growing all through the twenties, and the stock commuters that came along at the end of the decade from Chris-Craft, Gar Wood, Robinson, acf, Dodge, Luders, Hacker, and even Matthews and Wheeler, brought new players into a game that, like the roar of that great decade of wealth and promise, seemed guaranteed to go on forever. About thirty new commuters were launched in 1930, and most of them were custom-built. Meanwhile, the stock builders launched new models. In the magazines, American Car and Foundry (acf) advertised a 30-foot "cruiser runabout" with forward cockpit, a 38-foot twin-screw express yacht, and a 45-foot express commuter. During its brief fling with boatbuilding, this company that built railroad cars maintained showrooms in New York, Chicago, Boston, Cleveland, Detroit, San Francisco, and New Orleans. Robinson advertised its 39-foot sedan in two versions, one with a forward cockpit, and a 40-foot "Speed Cruiser" that looked very much like the Chris-Craft 38-foot commuters. The Horace E. Dodge Boat and Plane Corporation of Newport News introduced a new 45-foot Commuting Cruiser, a 35-mph boat with twin Lycoming V-12s for a price of $27,000 delivered at the plant in Virginia. Dodge also advertised limousine types in wonderful full-color ads in the magazines of the early thirties. Matthews developed a commuter version of its popular 38-footer for the 1930 season, along with a 46-foot double-cabin "Sport Cruiser" with forward cockpit, and Wheeler offered a similar 45-foot stock commuter. Huckins advertised its fast 45-footer as "the boat the stock market did not hurt." Lürssen of Germany, banned from exhibiting at the New York Motor Boat Show after World War I, displayed its wares at the 1930 show and built two big commuters for American owners in that first season after the stock market crash—a 75-footer and a 102-footer. Luders advertised its 72-foot streamlined Ludership commuter in 1930 but, hedging bets, seems to have given as much attention to a 42-footer capable of better than 25 mph, a slower boat than the 42-foot Luders stock commuters of the twenties. John Hacker advertised his high-speed marine limousines in the year he launched a mile-a-minute commuter for the king of Siam, and the Hacker Boat Company continued to advertise such boats for the rest of the decade. Gar Wood did the same, offering sedan and limousine types until 1941. Like Hacker, Gar Wood's main business was quick, elite runabouts for summer cottagers, along with a commuter or two when he could find a customer. But unlike Hacker the gray fox of Algonac's boatbuilding was subsidised in hard times by the steady profits of his dump-truck business. Chris-Craft, as noted, abandoned commuters after 1931 and promoted a line of cheaper runabouts and launches. Gar Wood and Hacker followed suit, selling boats priced under $1,000 throughout the 1930s with enough success to stay in business, although Hacker soon lost control of his company and even lost his house in St. Clair Shores.

But all was not gloom as the Depression wore on and many of the great commuters of the 1920s and early 1930s appeared in the brokerage pages of the magazines at bargain prices. Impressive custom boats were still built for some of the same people who ordered custom coachwork for Lincoln, Packard, and Cadillac limousines and touring cars in the 1930s, that great decade of classic automobiles. Robinson continued to build floating limousines during the decade, never finding enough customers but resisting the smarter move into cheaper launches and runabouts. And Consolidated and Purdy launched some of the great commuters of the 1930s. This book's Commuter Register, not guaranteed to be complete or even completely accurate, shows that Consolidated built fifty-one commuters during the Roaring Twenties and sixteen during the less-lively thirties. The Purdy brothers built eight commuters, among other fast and interesting boats, during the 1920s; in the 1930s the Purdy Boat Company built a dozen commuters, some of them the great ones.

The season of 1930 was a good one for Consolidated. Among commuters launched by the yard on the Harlem River were *Jem* for Jeremiah Milbank; the 75-foot *Cossack* for George Moffett; *Donmargo,* an 81-footer for C. E. Breen; *Pamnorm,* another 81-foot commuter for Norman Woolworth; the 75-foot *Reynard* for Thomas W. Lamont of New York; *Spitfire,* an 80-footer for the Reynoldson Company of New York and Stuart, Florida; and *Raider,* a 50-foot Tams and King design built for A. E. Walbridge of New York. The only survivor among these

1930 Consolidated products is *Jem,* now *Jessica,* discussed at some length in the previous chapter.

Subsequent years of the 1930s saw attrition in the commuter fleet altogether and in the building of these boats at Consolidated. The 55-foot *Lucky Strike* was built in 1931 for D. C. Hard of New York; in 1933 the 47-foot *Hawk* was built for G. J. Ottley, and *Sea Puss,* a 65-footer, was built for John T. Pratt. In 1934 the yard launched the 66-foot *Grey Gull* for W. S. Carpenter of Wilmington, Delaware. No more Consolidated commuters were built until 1937–38 when *Lancer,* a 65-foot Sparkman and Stephens design, was built for Ted Conover of Fort Lauderdale in 1937, and *Q.E.D.* and *Sea Bee III* were launched in 1938. *Sea Bee III* was a 54-foot commuter built for N. C. Atkinson of Philadelphia. *Q.E.D.* was one of the most spectacular yachts that Consolidated ever produced—a streamlined 112-foot blue torpedo designed by William Atkin for the aircraft genius Anthony Fokker. Atkin and Fokker collaborated on a construction scheme of African mahogany for the hull and lightweight aircraft plywood for interior structures, along with such innovations as a large mushroom anchor that was housed in the middle of the bottom. *Q.E.D.* was up-to-the-minute in specifications and style, and with twin Wright Typhoon engines of 600 hp apiece, plus a smaller Packard cruising engine, she was fast. But Fokker's *Q.E.D.* had a short career. In October of 1939 she burned and sank in the Hudson River with the loss of one of her crew.

The Purdy Boat Company built a small 35-foot commuter for Harold Vanderbilt in 1930, the year Vanderbilt defended the America's Cup from a challenge brought by Sir Thomas Lipton and the last of his *Shamrocks.* In 1931 the Purdys launched *Lady Nina,* a 72-footer for Charles Proctor, and *Miss Larchmont IV,* a fast 40-foot boat for Frank E. Campbell, Jr., of Larchmont, New York. In 1932, as mentioned earlier, the Purdys nearly lost the yard when their bank failed. Otherwise it was a pretty good year. Carl Fisher, their patron, had the 60-foot *Shadow Fay* built in 1932, and they also built *Skylark II,* a 65-foot commuter for Helen M. Smith, and *Corisande II,* another 65-footer, for Marshall Field. Like Consolidated, the Purdy Boat Com-

LUCKY STRIKE

A 55-foot Consolidated built in 1932 for A. E. Blackman of New Rochelle, New York. She is flying the owner's private signal and the burgee of the venerable Seawanhaka Corinthian Yacht Club of Oyster Bay, Long Island.

LUCKY STRIKE

The enclosed deckhouse and control station of the Consolidated-designed and built Lucky Strike. She had Consolidated Speedway engines and a Speedway instrument panel. Note the good visibility all around. Below, the comfortable interior of Lucky Strike.

Q.E.D.

This fabulous yacht-commuter was designed by William Atkin in conjunction with its owner, the legendary aircraft genius Tony Fokker. Built by Consolidated in 1938, she was state-of-the-art, composite construction. But she unfortunately burned and sank after two seasons' use. Flying the Netherlands national flag, she is shown here on the NYYC cruise in 1938.

SEA PUSS

A later, Consolidated-designed and built commuter for John T. Pratt, Jr. She was fast, powered by twin V-12 Wright Tornados, and had a more modern deck-house configuration.

MISS LARCHMONT IV

A snappy 1931 Purdy commuter built for Frank E. Campbell, Jr. Following in his father's footsteps, Frank Jr. had a number of high-speed boats built for his use on Long Island Sound. She flies the Larchmont burgee—what else?

pany had to wait for better times before launching its most spectacular creation, the 74-foot *Aphrodite III* for John Hay Whitney.

The history of Jock Whitney's third *Aphrodite* is bound up with the history of Charles Shipman Payson's *Saga*, the commuter I owned in the 1960s. *Saga* was built for Payson, Jock's brother-in-law. He had married Jock's sister Joan, who eventually owned the New York Mets baseball team, and the Whitneys and Paysons lived on adjoining Long Island estates. They were rivals, and *Saga* was built in 1935 by Wheeler to be a faster commuter than Jock Whitney's second *Aphrodite*, a 72-foot Albany Boat Works product built in 1928. *Aphrodite II* was not a lucky boat, and her performance was improved by Consolidated in the early 1930s—but not enough to rival the flashing speed of *Saga*. With her twin 750-hp V-12 aircraft conversions, the new *Saga* consistently humbled Whitney's commuter in their daily runs in and out of New York in 1935 and 1936. Jock Whitney, a man hardly ever at a loss, had the Purdy Boat Company build *Aphrodite III* in 1936–37 specifically to beat *Saga*.

Aphrodite III not only outpaced her rival in the late 1930s, she survived everything from hard use under Jock Whitney and his captain, John Stroehr, to hard times under indifferent owners in the 1960s and 1970s. From 1937 to 1962, *Aphrodite* led a fast and happy life, delivering her owner to the city and to other destinations up and down the coast, taking movie stars and other celebrities for boat rides and cruises as Jock's guests, delivering classified documents to Franklin Roosevelt and doing patrol duty as a Coast Guard boat during World War II.

Whitney gave *Aphrodite* to a boy's camp on Long Island in 1962, and from there she passed through several owners, one of whom kept pet goats aboard. She had deteriorated almost past saving by the early 1980s, sinking several times in a boatyard at the end of Long Island and finally being put ashore with sprung planks, ruined machinery, and accelerating rot in her once-dazzling Mexican mahogany. Then she was found by John Pannell, owner of the Harbor View Marina in Port Washington, Long Island—a boatyard on the site of the old Purdy Boat Company where *Aphrodite* had been built. Pannell

APHRODITE III

The graceful Aphrodite on her trial run shortly after she was completed. She probably was not fully commissioned at this time. It appears that the Purdy brothers are aboard and the tall man at the helm could be the owner, Jack Whitney. Her hull was first painted a pearl gray, then later a gloss black. Here we see a good example of the "Purdy bow."

acquired this great commuter—and daunting restoration project—in 1984, and he and his crew put more than ten thousand hours into bringing her back. *Aphrodite* is now as good as new from clipper bow to tapered stern, and she has been an exciting sight in East Coast waters and at antique-boat gatherings from Florida to Canada since the middle of the 1980s.

Another outstanding survivor from the thirties commuter fleet is *Marlin*, noted earlier and built by the Lawley yard in 1930 for Edsel Ford as a dual-purpose commuter and sportfishing boat. *Marlin*—51′6″ × 12′6″ beam × 3′ draft—was designed by Walter McInnis with trim patrol-boat lines, bright-finished Honduras mahogany on her hull and house, and twin 245-hp Sterling Dolphin engines for a top speed of 28 mph. Notable features are a large forward cockpit, cabin amidships with sleeping accommodations for four people, a large after cockpit arranged for fishing with chairs, fish well and bait well under the cockpit sole. The after cockpit is fitted with auxiliary steering and engine controls. *Marlin* originally carried an 8-foot Lyman skiff on the after part of the house, and extending several feet from her plumb bow was a swordfishing-style pulpit.

Although not arranged like *Marlin*, three similar boats were designed by Walter McInnis—*Lindale, Bonito II,* and *Pronto.* Edsel Ford was almost as frugal as his father and had sold his commuter *Greyhound* for $30,000 prior to taking delivery of *Marlin,* sight unseen, fully commissioned in Miami. He had been aboard *Bonito II* and, impressed, asked Walter McInnis to design something similar. *Marlin* was the third of the series. Her career after Edsel Ford sold her in 1935 is a bit vague, but she was owned in the late 1930s by Arthur Houghton of the Corning Glass Corporation, and by the Schenley distilling company, and she saw service with the Coast Guard in World War II, patrolling between Palm Beach and Fort Lauderdale. After the war she was owned by the Yellow Cab Company.

In 1952, while languishing in a boatyard in Falmouth on Cape Cod, *Marlin* was bought by Joseph P. Kennedy. Joe Kennedy inspected the boat in company with Walter McInnis. *Marlin* was a bit neglected,

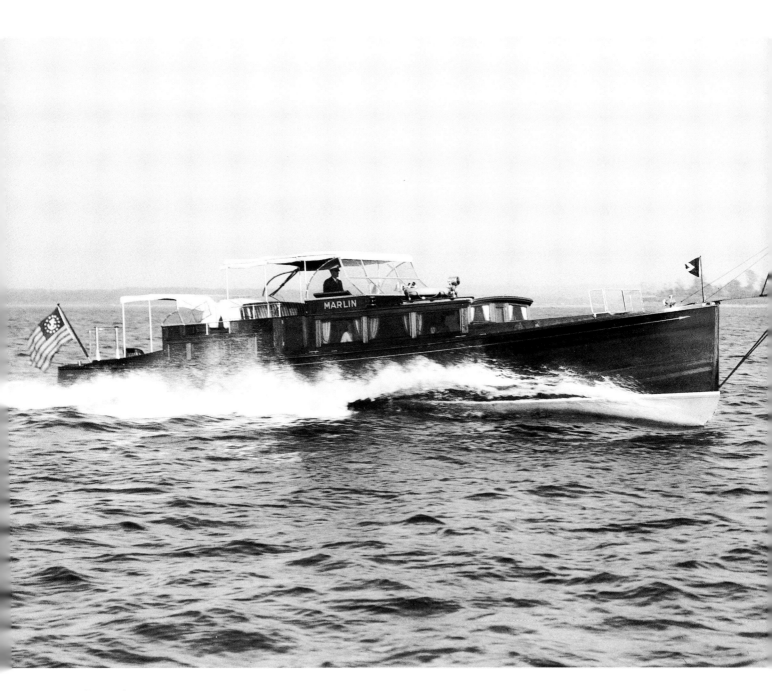

MARLIN (DEAMA)

The historic Lawley commuter—built for Edsel Ford and later owned by Kennedy family—shown in her original configuration with bow pulpit and aft controls above transom. One of five of Walter McInnis's notable designs of this type, she is the beloved cruiser of the Acierno family, and attended the Commuters 1991 rendezvous.

and the father of the future president agreed with Walter's suggestions for work to be done but balked at the additional cost of new diesel engines to replace the Chrysler Royal gas engines that were in her. She served the Kennedys for many years, and became an unofficial presidential yacht. In 1961 we were going north with *Saga* on Lake Worth in Palm Beach and were fortunate to see *Marlin* with President and Mrs. Kennedy aboard. After much frantic waving by the five offspring rushing back and forth on *Saga*, both Kennedys waved back and my two girls just about collapsed with joy.

Currently *Marlin* is in the capable hands of the Acierno family on Long Island. Except for newer Chrysler V8s, she is mostly in original condition, and during the season she is out most weekends fishing and day-cruising. She joined the fleet of Commuters '91 in Oyster Bay, New York City, on Long Island Sound and the Connecticut River, and at Mystic Seaport's annual July antique-boat show.

Other outstanding commuters of the 1930s included John Hacker designs for the 54-foot *Ravelston*, built in 1939 by Huskins Boat Company of Bay City, Michigan; the 83-foot *Restless*, built by Defoe in 1933 for D. T. Wende of Buffalo; *Wee Joe II*, a 55-foot Hacker/Huskins collaboration built in 1939 for Joe Cooper; and the 44-foot *Tempo*, built by Huskins for Guy Lombardo, who commuted in her to his concerts at Jones Beach on Long Island. *Ravelston*, a stunning boat with contrasting patterns of grain in her mahogany planking, is restored and owned now in Canada. Robinson of Michigan built some of its biggest and most impressive commuters in the 1930s, including the 56-foot *Judith R.* for Barney Balaban of New London, Connecticut, the 50-foot *Joaneda* for R. B. Anderson of Boston, and *Harbel*, a 48-footer for Harvey Firestone.

Between the end of the Depression (whenever it ended) and the beginning of World War II, only a few commuters were built—certainly a portent. Charles Payson ordered a new *Saga* from Sparkman and Stephens, a 53-footer built in 1941 by the Quincy Adams yard in Boston, and David Gerli of Smithtown, Long Island, had the 76-foot *Paratus* designed by John Wells and built by Julius Peterson in 1941. In 1940 one of John Hacker's greatest creations, the 55-foot *Thun-*

derbird, was built by Huskins in Michigan and shipped by railroad to Lake Tahoe for George Whittell, who commuted in her around the big lake. She later became part of Bill Harrah's world-renowned collection of cars and boats, and under new owners *Thunderbird* can still be seen and heard on Lake Tahoe. With her varnished mahogany hull and stainless-steel deckhouse she can be seen reflecting the California sun as she moves along at more than 60 mph, and with twin 1,000-hp Allison V-12 aircraft engines she can definitely be heard.

World War II interrupted boatbuilding and much else until late in the 1940s. Yacht commuting, that phenomenon of the exciting twenties that survived against all odds through the hard times of the thirties, would decline precipitously in the postwar world. Finally it would be all but gone—but not forgotten.

HALL BY HERSELF
Built by the Purdy brothers for Carl Fisher in 1924 and shown after being recommissioned twelve years later, Hall by Herself *has unique owner's scrollwork at her bow and flies an owner's signal on the mast and Larchmont Yacht Club burgee from bow.*

TEMPO

A well-known commuter designed by Charles D. Mower and built by Henry Nevins. Owned by the famous band leader and race-boat competitor, Guy Lombardo, she is shown dressed out with Lombardo's private signal and Red Bank Yacht Club burgee. Below: At the motorboat races in Red Bank, New Jersey, with her famous owner aboard.

EPEE

A magnificent Long Island Sound commuter used for many years by the Plant family. Designed and built by Luders shipyard in 1929. Her deckhouse treatment is typical Luders. She had a small forward cockpit and twin Sterling engines.

VOLKERTSE

One of the few commuters designed by William Atkin. Built by Chute and Bixby of Long Island in 1932. She had the forerunner of the radar arch and was powered by Sterlings.

VOLKERTSE

The flying bridge control station. The transmission gear-shift levers to starboard of the wheel could be a problem in some docking conditions. Below: Not much room in the engine room with a pair of matched Consolidated Speedway flat-head sixes. The generator can be seen over the starboard engine.

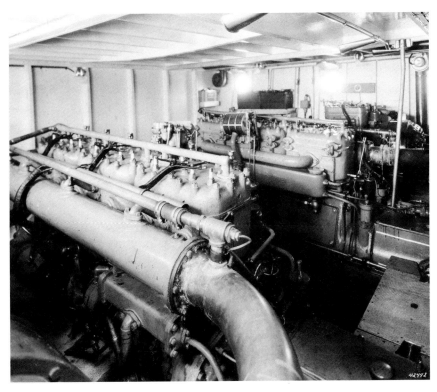

VAMPIRE

Ralph Pulitzer's fast Tams and King–designed Nevins-built commuter, shown running on the Sound, flying the Pulitzer private signal, owner's absent flag, and the pennant of the Manhasset Bay Yacht Club. She is much like Phantom and Whim.

VENUS

One of the sharp, 42-foot Luders Marine Construction commuters shown running up the Hudson. About six or seven of these attractive, Sterling-powered craft were turned out. The nicely faired forward cockpit is noticeable. She is flying the owner's private signal, owner's absent flag, and Colonial (Hudson River, Manhattan), Yacht Club flags.

JOANEDA

One of the Robinson Seagull commuters of the 1930s. The Robinson Marine Construction Company of Benton Harbor, Michigan, built a series of these attractive 40 to 50 foot commuters, almost on a production basis, and usually powered with twin Hall-Scott 6-cylinder Invaders.

PROTEST

This is a nice Dyer Motorcraft commuter of 38 feet, launched for Allen Lindley of New York in 1929. A compact commuter with full accommodations. Powered with twin Kermaths.

YAP YAP

A handsome 40-foot Robinson Seagull commuter shown at the Detroit running of the British International motorboat races in 1933. Powered by two Kermath 225 hp 6-cylinders, she could attain 42 mph. Her owner, Victor Kliesrath, was a Gold Cup driver.

YAP YAP

The control station and engine room. The big Kermath Sea Wolves were about the largest twin engine installation in the 42-foot production boat. Below: the main cabin looking forward, with opening windows on the sides. The cocktail shaker and service was probably for show. Seat backs could be attached to the overhead to create upper bunks.

TANGO

A 45-foot production commuter from the Seagull line of the Robinson Marine Construction Company of Benton Harbor, Michigan. Powered by twin Hall-Scotts, they were competitors of Chris-Craft and acf.

WEE JOE II

Classic John Hacker–designed commuter, built by Huskins Boat Company, Bay City, Michigan. Clean, low lines, covered her forward cockpit. Built in 1937.

AVOCA

One of the last commuters built by Herreshoff for the avid Connecticut yachtsman E. E. Dickinson, Jr. from a smooth Sparkman and Stephens design. A fast 66-footer, she is flying the burgee of the Dauntless Club of Connecticut.

BLACKBIRD

A Cox and Stevens design built by Julius Peterson at Nyack, New York. This 94-footer carries two deck boats and seems to be dressed out for some 1930s regatta off New London, Connecticut.

BLACKBIRD

Her deckhouse is typical of a commuter of the 1930s. A writing desk, chairs, and sofa of the period can be seen. Below: Looking forward in the dining space of Blackbird. The photograph was taken right after commissioning and she looked sort of spare. Underfoot is the latest thing—linoleum.

BLACKBIRD:

Accommodations below. Guests slept in comfort although these early photographs show an unlived-in state.

BLACKBIRD

Typical galley and crews quarters on an 80- to 90-foot commuter of late 1920s. The galley would not be tolerated even on a 30-foot express cruiser in today's world. Right: Blackbird head with full bath.

BLACKBIRD

The comfortable cockpit just aft of the helm station. Three deck boats are in place and a davit for landing stage is on the far left. Below: Wicker furniture was both stylish in the era and helped keep weight at a minimum.

BLACKBIRD
The straightforward control station. Only the essential controls are in the pilothouse; the main instrument panel is in the engine room. Below: This photo of the engine room is looking aft at the matched pair of gasoline Wintons. Tools and chainfalls are ready for use. Full controls for the engines are at hand as engineer was stationed close by.

GEREDNA

A nicely proportioned 72-foot Luders owned in the 1930s by J. H. Higgins, with Luders Marine Construction scrollwork at bow. Shown in the East River with uniformed crew, she is flying her owner's signal, the owner's absent flag, and the Indian Harbor Yacht Club burgee from her bow staff.

GEREDNA
Covered "back porch" with comfortable wicker furniture. Below: The main dining space of Geredna. Her galley is forward and down below.

153

GEREDNA

The main saloon with a fold-down table, and ladder to the vessel's main dining room. Below: The aft stateroom showing the hand-painted writing desk and elaborate curtains. Storage drawers are under the beds and the ladder leads to the "back porch."

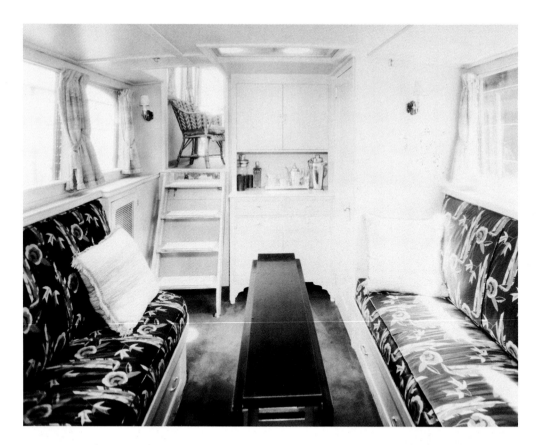

GEREDNA

A no frills galley. Note side arm hot water heater and latest in chrome toasters. Left: Looking forward in the engine room. The matched pair of Sterling 8-cylinder Dolphins of 300 hp pushed Geredna at a 28-mph speed.

155

Chapter Five

Decline and Revival

ELITE YACHT BUILDERS DID NOT SURVIVE WELL IN THE POSTWAR world. Some chose not even to wait until peacetime shortages of both materials and well-heeled customers did them in. With a statement from Carl Haffenreffer, general manager, the great Herreshoff yard closed its doors in late 1944: "Because manpower, materials, and price restrictions prevent Herreshoff from entering civilian production for some time to come, it is with regret that we find it necessary to disband our efficient and loyal organization and to dispose of our facilities at Bristol . . ." The Lawley yard built its last boat in 1946—for the U.S. Navy. Gar Wood and Robinson went out of business in 1948. The Purdy Boat Company was just another boatyard by 1950. Consolidated built its last yacht at Morris Heights in 1948, then set up in smaller facilities on City Island until 1956 when a fire destroyed the plant. Luders and Hacker lasted longer—the former building small stock boats in wood until the mid-1960s, and the Hacker boat company surviving on speedboat building until 1956. acf and Dodge were long gone by the 1950s. Chris-Craft survived nicely in an unpre-

ROCK BOTTOM

A later commuter designed in 1950 by Raymond Hunt for Roger Firestone of Philadelphia pictured here in 1951 flying the Jolly Roger and the pennant of the Atlantic Tuna Club. Built by the Quincy Adams yard in Quincy, Massachusetts, this 42-footer was first powered by a single V-12 Packard for thrilling speeds. In 1954 twin Grays were installed.

DAUNTLESS

An impressive Sparkman and Stephens design for Laurance Rockefeller, this postwar commuter was built in 1947 with an aluminum hull by Jakobson Shipyard of Oyster Bay, Long Island. With two V-12 Packards, she still commutes on the Hudson.

dictable new boating market, building everything from plywood kit boats to the big Constellations of the fifties, and became in that decade of middle-class prosperity the greatest producer of recreational boats in the world.

These builders of commuters and express yachts faced shortages of boatbuilding wood and other materials, shortages of capital, even shortages of new ideas after the war. Most of all they experienced a lack of customers for elite machines such as commuters. Yacht commuting began with the great financial manipulators of the 1880s and 1890s, continued through World War I with prosperity and the status value of owning a yacht, took off during the 1920s with a new generation of men who had new money along with a passion for commuting to work in big planing yachts that were also new, then declined during the 1930s as the new money disappeared and only some of the old money remained secure enough for such an indulgence as riding and often racing to work in a boat that cost as much to run every week as the average mechanic made in a month. It seems that the very rich started it all, then had imitators as long as the money lasted. After 1930, the phenomenon of yacht commuting—and it was nothing less than a phenomenon during the Jazz Age—was left for the very rich to carry on. After World War II, a new generation of the very rich or the very self-indulgent chose not to carry on—with a few exceptions.

There were some new commuters built after the war, even as the old commuting yachts became cruising boats or liveaboards and began their disappearances in the corners of old boatyards or on river mudbanks. *Makaira*, a 70-foot Trumpy, was built in 1946 for Les Sears of Palm Beach, and *Sea Puss II*, a 55-foot successor to the 65-foot *Sea Puss I* built in 1933 by Consolidated, was delivered to John T. Pratt by Consolidated in 1946. *Pardon Me*, the awesome 47-foot Hacker-designed commuter for Charles P. Lyon of the Thousand Islands, was built in 1947 by the Hutchinson Boat Works; Luders launched the 82-foot *Bengal* in 1947 for Arthur Wellman, Jr., of Boston; the 58-foot *Goddess* was built for Richard du Pont in 1947 by Consolidated; and Mrs. Winthrop Bradley of Long Island had the 33-foot *Laughing Lady* built by Luders in 1947 for trips between Gardiners Island and

Southampton. *Pardon Me,* a boat so mechanically fussy that Charlie Lyon hardly ever used her, is now in the collection of the Antique Boat Museum in Clayton, New York, thanks to Jim Lewis, who bought and donated this significant Thousand Islands boat. With a 1500-hp Packard PT-Boat engine drinking quantities of aviation fuel, *Pardon Me* is capable of more than 50 mph; but in her first few seasons she proved difficult in close quarters, with erratic hydraulic shifting and a too-small rudder, and her engine was prone to overheating. *Pardon Me* became Dick Locke's *Lockpat III* in 1950 in Detroit, and was acquired by Nick Beck in the mid-1970s. Beck restored this huge speedboat and solved her mechanical problems. As for *Bengal,* she was last seen in the late 1980s as a floating bed and breakfast in Fernandina Beach, Florida.

In 1949 the 60-foot *Alva* was built by Trumpy for Colonel E. E. Dickinson, Jr.; the 65-foot *Dauntless* was built in aluminum by the Jakobson Shipyard for Laurance Rockefeller; the 42-foot *Sea Blitz* was built by Graves Yacht Yard for Bradley Noyes of Boston; *Skytop II,* a 52-foot Consolidated, was built for Richard Gould of Miami Beach; and the first *Cassiar,* a 64-foot boat designed by Ben Dobson and built by Palmer Scott, was delivered to Lt. General Richard K. Mellon, who kept her in Woods Hole. *Sea Blitz* was another postwar boat with a 1500-hp Packard PT-Boat engine, and her hull was an early part of the evolution of the deep-V hull that Ray Hunt perfected in the late 1950s. Laurance Rockefeller's *Dauntless,* designed by Sparkman and Stephens, had two Packard engines of the PT type—2,700 total horsepower for a speed of 40 knots.

Only a few new commuters came along in the 1950s. Arthur Vining Davis took delivery of his 52-foot *Elda,* built in Germany by Krogerwerft in 1954, and commuted in her from Miami to his real estate projects in the Bahamas. *Sands of Time,* a 47-foot Dutch-built Feadship, was delivered to William Bradford of Falmouth, Massachusetts, in 1956, and a familiar 1950s commuter in Miami was the 32-foot *Black Caesar,* built by Forest Johnson for Bob Collins in 1957. By 1960, yacht commuting was practically dead in the United States, although a few very rich Europeans still considered a yacht the best transportation for some business travel and for port-to-port sprints in the Mediterranean, where roads were clogged with traffic in the high season. Stavros Niarchos used his 102-foot *Mercury*, designed by Peter DuCane and built by Vosper in England in 1960, for high-speed commuting in the Med, and Gianni Agnelli, chairman of Fiat, had several commuters designed by Renato Levi at his disposal in the 1960s. Agnelli's first Levi-designed commuter was *Ultima Dea*, a 36-footer built of laminated mahogany in 1962, and fitted with head, galley, dinette, and berths for five. Powered by three 430-hp Maserati V8s with double overhead camshafts—a total of twelve camshafts and twelve double Weber carburetors—*Ultima Dea* was about the ultimate rough-water flyer, capable of 50 mph. She was also an offshore racer that competed in England's Cowes-Torquay race. *G. Cinquanta*, the Agnelli family's 1968 commuter, was a needle-nosed offshore-racing type powered by four 320-hp engines for speeds close to 60 knots. On these shores, a 53-foot Huckins built in 1962, a boat I acquired some years later as *Quicksilver*, was used by her second owner as a commuter between Pompano Beach and Miami. And in the postwar years there were island commuters in places like New York State's Thousand Islands and the San Juan Islands of the Pacific Northwest.

Aircraft and helicopters served executive travelers increasingly in the postwar world. They were faster than the quickest of the flyers, and the postwar world was a faster track for business than even the twenties had been. Yacht commuting was considered old-fashioned and self-indulgent.

When the revival of interest in these boats began is hard to define, but the new phenomenon of commuter acquisition and restoration has certainly been a result of the antique and classic boat movement in general, and of two recent gatherings of commuters in particular.

The old-boat movement began in the 1960s with the first boat show devoted to antique and classic boats taking place at what was then the Thousand Islands Shipyard Museum in Clayton, New York, in 1965. The museum has recently changed its name to the Antique Boat Museum, and its collection has grown with the movement. By 1974 there were antique-boat clubs at the Thousand Islands museum and in Detroit. There were clubs for Elco, Matthews and Richardson cruisers, a Chris-Craft Antique Boat Club, an Antique Outboard Motor Club, and active clubs in Canada and in the West collecting, restoring, and displaying old boats at annual gatherings. In the summer of 1974, vintage-boat enthusiasts gathered for the first annual Lake George Antique and Classic Boat Rendezvous, and nine of them got excited about something they proposed to call the Antique and Classic Boat Society. On January 25, 1975, they incorporated, adopted a constitution and bylaws, and started what has become the principal organization in the old-boat hobby. By 1977 the ACBS had 400 members, and it grew to more than 1,000 members by 1980, to 2,200 members by 1983, and to more than 4,000 members in the early 1990s. The membership renewal rate is over 80 percent, and activities include boat shows, maintenance workshops, historical sessions, newsletters, and various social events year-round. In 1987, the nefarious Commuter Captains Club was founded in Fargo, North Dakota, as a commuter complement to the growing number of clubs and ACBS chapters. Very little can be reported of this singular organization except that it began with an original group of eccentric commuter enthusiasts and connoisseurs to bring a bit of levity to the ever-more-serious business of antique boating.

In August of 1989, two of North America's foremost antique-boating organizations, what was then the Thousand Islands Shipyard Museum, and Canada's Manotick Classic Boat Club, launched the first of what will surely be periodic gatherings of restored commuters. With Mike Matheson, Bob MacKay, Frank Phelan, and the author as organizers, Commuters '89 began during the 24th edition of the Clayton show that started it all. It was suggested that the commuters could rendezvous at Clayton for the Thousand Islands show, take off for a midweek cruise up the Rideau system, then enjoy a second antique-boat gathering in the Manotick club's territory in Ottawa.

Invitations were sent out, and ten commuters or near-commuters showed up at the Clayton docks for the well-organized, laid-back, 126-mile passage up the beautiful Rideau canal and waterway system to the Canadian capital. As stern linesman and fender-offer ("Fend off the stern, Phil; we're coming in on the port side of this next lock") on Jim and Toni Lewis's *Mavourneen*, the author had a great opportunity to observe these elegant boats commuting to Ottawa. Along with *Mavourneen* were commuters of every size, from the 22-foot *Jolly Roger* to the stately 75-foot *Jessica*. Seeing Captain Thombs maneuver *Jessica* through the narrows between the Rideau lakes with literally inches to spare was a lesson in helmsmanship and astute judgment. Even with the 9-foot beam of *Mavourneen*, we had to back and fill more than once to get around some of the tight bends. Locking through the Rideau system was looked upon with some apprehension by most of the skippers, as the 160-year old locks are solid limestone and sandstone blocks, fitted with massive oak gates that are replaced from time to time, and operated like big bathtub toys with water let in and let out to meet the level above or below. The sluice gates are controlled by the same iron-cog-and-chain winches and other machinery installed by Colonel John By, the English engineer who created the Rideau system from a network of swamps, streams, and boggy lakes more than 150 years ago. All of this is manually operated in the summers by college students in khaki shirts and shorts, male and female, who crank the handles with a will and seem to enjoy it. Overseeing the locks is a professional staff headed by John Bonser, an English-Canadian engineer who holds the title of Superintendent of the Rideau Canal and who joined Commuters '89 for the trip through his locks, coming aboard different boats at different times. After the second lock, all skippers and hands became accustomed to the routine of sorting out boats, fenders, and lines for the thirty-five remaining locks to Dow's Lake in Ottawa. The Rideau Waterway, constructed between 1826 and 1832 on the advice of the Duke of Wellington, has forty-nine locks in all.

We traveled through single locks and flights of locks with efficiency and in-the-locks cameraderie. In the locks, once things settled down and the pace of water on the rise was comfortable, people in different boats gammed and visited aboard. In one of the lower locks one of our braver crew members, Jane Remington, dove into the water to retrieve an errant fender. She was greeted with hearty applause as she climbed back aboard. As we wound our way northeast, the old-boat lovers of the Manotick club were the perfect hosts. One evening we were all ferried out to Don and Marlene Thomas's plantation-like estate for a delightful outdoor dinner. As we approached Ottawa we were welcomed in the Manotick club's "Mahogany Harbour," named for the many beautiful antique boats that have been kept in this Ottawa suburb for generations.

At Mahogany Harbour we met all the members of the club, and after all the boats were docked we were treated to a party at Syd and Mary Herwig's waterfront home—sponsored, as was the whole of Commuters '89, by Schweppes and Amstel and Tilley Endurables, builders of those rakish Canadian boating hats. The breakfast on Friday morning at Murray and Sarah Gould's house was a great beginning for the day—in fact, for the weekend—at Dow's Lake Pavilion in Ottawa. Hundreds of the people of this impressive city turned out to welcome the commuters as they came into town. We were a show for them and they were a show for us. This is a city that has made the most of its landscape and its waterways—the Rideau River, the Ottawa River, the Rideau Canal—and cruising through it is like cruising through a garden. There are parks and there are walled sections with esplanades along the water, walkways and bicycle paths and summer greenery draping down the stone walls, elegant bridges and public buildings. On Saturday night aboard the Thousand Islands Shipyard Museum's commuter *Zipper* we cruised in the dark past a baseball stadium lit for a night game, past lively restaurants on the canal, past the esplanades softly lit and full of strollers. On Sunday we visited the old market section of the city, full of summer produce and crowds of Canadians speaking French and English. Ottawa is a city that shows us what an "urban environment" is supposed to be. Commuters '89 was a great success, just as wonderful as it is briefly described here—so much so that a second gathering of commuters began to be planned, possibly bigger and better and located in the old commuter territory of New York and Long Island Sound.

The 1991 commuter rendezvous, which included an authentic dash down the East River to Wall Street with business executives aboard, began on a misty morning at Essex, Connecticut, on July 22, 1991. We left the Connecticut River on a hot, foggy, and humid morning aboard Mike and Anne Matheson's 38-foot Chris-Craft commuter *Tradition* for the run down and across Long Island Sound to the venerable Seawanhaka Corinthian Yacht Club on Oyster Bay. There we were to rendezvous with the rest of the commuter fleet. Of the twenty or so invited, eleven of the old flyers showed up. Three of the lovely old Consolidateds—*Jessica, Miss Asia,* and *Ragtime*—cruised the entire distance. Of the five Chris-Craft commuters, four made the run. Edsel Ford's old *Marlin,* now named *Deama,* completed the cruise along with the black-hulled *Annie Laurie,* a 1929 commuter type built in Maine and recently restored by Barry White of Old Saybrook, Connecticut. After tying up 487 feet of commuters at the limited dock space, a fine dinner was laid on in the old club's dining room. Air-conditioning was not part of the program at Seawanhaka in the 1890s or now, and the 95-degree temperature didn't help. But with various liquid coolers in the charming atmosphere we survived it well enough.

The following morning we got our bearings and after hearing reports that severe storms and even a tornado watch were predicted for later in the day, we departed for the run to South Street Seaport in lower Manhattan, where our commuting executives would take off for Wall Street. This was almost like the glory days of commuting down the East River, although at a much-reduced pace as the day was balmy and there was some great scenery. The facilities at South Street Seaport leave something to be desired for commuters. Among the historic harbor vessels and two big grain-trade windjammers tied up along the high granite pier, even *Jessica* was almost lost. The Seaport did provide floating docks with a ladder. The climb up the ladder—about 40 feet—and then over the railings was one of the high points of Commuters '91. The author understands that awards are to be presented to some of the ladies for their valiant efforts in ascending the "Seaport staircase."

After a short, interesting tour and an ethnic lunch, we departed the Seaport about two in the afternoon for a 50-mile run to Port Jefferson on the north shore of Long Island for an overnight stay at Danforth's Inn and Marina. Once we left the East River we picked up speed on *Tradition* as there were ominous black clouds moving slowly across the Sound from Connecticut. We were running about 25 knots in a lumpy seaway with the wind increasing. Visibility was decreasing at an alarming rate due to the blowing rain squalls. With everyone down below except Mike Matheson and the navigator—the author, who had grown up on the Sound, and in a weak moment had volunteered—things began getting worse. On the open bridge it was hard enough to see the chart let alone anything much in front of the boat. For a fleeting instant we caught sight of the buoy off Port Jefferson, then all hell broke loose with the full fury of the storm catching us as we swung to starboard and surfed downwind toward the jetties.

As we got inside, the wind gusts at 40 and 50 mph were blowing everything around—hanging flower containers were blowing away, flags were ripping apart, boats were hobbyhorsing at their moorings. The Coast Guard boat with flashing blue lights went charging out as it rapidly got darker. The flying spray eased somewhat as we slowly proceeded to the docks, then all the lights at the marina and in town went out. *Tradition* managed to get in and tie up, but some of the boats following were caught out in it. Two commuters took shelter in other harbors. *Jessica* was the last one to dock. Captain Thombs, with the boat for forty-five years, said he had been in only "one or two storms that were worse." Later, after skippers and crews reached port and sorted things out, some hair-raising stories were told—of sudden big seas, damage aboard, just hanging on. Evidently this was not just another summer storm on Long Island Sound.

The next day was bright and sunny, and the run across the Sound was uneventful. The fleet cruised up the Connecticut River to Essex and the Connecticut River Museum where the museum staff hosted a dockside reception. The day after, in a light rain, we made the "Run to Mystic," a free-for-all at full throttle for the 20 miles. It was a memorable sight to see nine of these classic express yachts running at almost flank speed. The four 38-foot Chris-Crafts were in the lead, one or two doing over 30 knots.

The commuter fleet was met at the entrance to Fishers Island Sound by Mystic Seaport's tugboat *Kingston II,* and a film crew began capturing the epic event for a documentary on commuters. The following day was a blast from the past with the 16th annual Mystic Seaport Antique and Classic Boat Rendezvous where the commuters were the main attraction. All fifty-six participating yachts paraded up and down the river with the dazzling commuters leading the fleet. Each boat was saluted in turn by the Seaport's impressive steamboat *Sabino,* where much partying was in progress accompanied by a jazz band.

Commuters '91 was a resounding success for both the hardworking, storm-wracked, but happy participants and for the interested and appreciative spectators on shore. There will be more of these gatherings.

A few new commuters and commuter types have come along since the revival began sometime in the 1970s. In 1975 the Stroh brewing family had the 43-foot *Zipper* built by Les Staudacher from plans for a Stroh family commuter that was never built. *Zipper* was a Purdy design, and has all the Purdy trademarks—lovely sheerline, tumble-home stern, canoe-like curve to the bow. She is now in the collection of the Antique Boat Museum in Clayton, New York. The first of the Tom Fexas–designed Midnight Lace express cruisers—new commuter types with slim hull forms and forward cockpits—was built in 1979 for Jim Lewis, and more were built in the 1970s and 1980s. At the famous Cutts and Case Shipyard in Oxford, Maryland, a brand-new 65-foot commuter is under construction using Ed Cutts's patented method of lightweight double planking reinforced with Kevlar cord. Cutts promises that his *Americana,* when launched, will weigh only 15,000 pounds with all her machinery and Spanish-cedar joinery.

In East Boothbay, Maine the venerable Hodgdon Brothers Yard is building to contract a modern version of *Saga*. Designed by Bruce King, she will be powered by twin V-12 M.A.N. diesels. At about 35 knots and 80′ long × 15′ beam, she will be an exciting addition to the commuter fleet. The launching is expected sometime in 1995.

There are about fifty of the old commuters still around, of which about a dozen are restored and in commission. At least another dozen are in the restoration process. Larry Lewis, son of Jim Lewis who has done so much for the world of classic boats in general and for the Antique Boat Museum in particular, had two commuters in restoration in the summer of 1992 at his shop in Mount Dora, Florida. Mike Matheson's Biscayne Bay Boat Works, with facilities in Mount Dora and in Murphy, North Carolina, delivered a restored commuter in 1991 and has three more in progress. Other old flyers are being rebuilt and refinished by individual owners, and still others—more than a few, we would hope—wait to be found and brought back to life. And the king of Siam's 60-mph John Hacker commuter is in storage in Bangkok, part of the royal family's collection of boats and automobiles.

The glory days of yacht commuting appear to be over, but many of these yachts in a hurry still thrill visitors to antique-boat gatherings and satisfy their owners with flashing speed, the essential elegance of the express yachts of yesteryear, and the satisfaction of bringing an exciting bit of yachting history to life again.

Commuter Register

The register of commuters includes the name of the commuter, owner's name and residence, designer and builder, dimensions, source of information, and when known, original engines as well as the year and location of construction. With a particularly significant commuter, a brief summary and history are included. In a few cases the same commuter is listed under more than one name.

Although it is impossible to make the register of commuters complete, almost 400 power craft are listed. In a loose sense of the word, all the craft in the register were commuters although some boats were not used or built for this purpose. They are included as a result of their similarities in hull design and construction, power, and speed. Some craft go far beyond the simple definition of a commuter and are included as the super- or maxi-commuters of their time.

All efforts have been made to provide complete information regarding each commuter. In some cases certain information was not available, and this is indicated by an incomplete listing (as, for example, when complete dimensions are not known), or the initials n/a (not available).

NAME	OWNER	DESIGNER/BLDR	DIMENSIONS	ENGINE	SPEED	SOURCE
ADA H.	K. Ames Jacksonville, FL	Robinson Seagull Benton Harbor, MI 1930	45′ × 10′	2 Hall-Scotts	35 mph	Y 5-'30 P-Ad
ADIOS II	A.E. Fitkin New York, NY	T.D. Bowles/ Mathis Shipbuilding Camden, NJ 1927	56′ × 11′	2 Speedways	52 mph	Y 11-'27 Pic.
ALIDA	B.H. Borden New York, NY	Consolidated Morris Heights, NY 1929	75′ × 12′10″ × 3′6″	2 6-cyl Speedways	20 mph	Consol Ad Lloyds '31
ALEGRETTO Gee Gee Rima	R.W. Green, Jr. Ft. Lauderdale, FL	G. Lawley & Son Neponset, MA 1926	68′ × 12′6″ × 3′8″	2 Hall-Scotts	20 mph	CPM 6-'62
ALERT	A. Schwarzler n/a	Purdy Boat Co. Port Washington, NY 1927	45′ × 10′	2 6-cyl 300-hp Scripps	34 mph	Y 2-'30 P R 10-'29
ALVA	E.E. Dickinson, Jr. Essex, CT	Sparkman & Stephens/ Trumpy Annapolis, MD 1949	60′ × 16′ × 3′6″	2 Hall-Scotts	n/a	MB 1-'50 Lloyds '62
ALTONIA	A.C. Newby Miami, FL	Purdy Boat Co. Miami Beach, FL 1919	46′ × 9′ Hull #33	2 Speedways	30 mph	Y 11-'71 R 4-'20

(Similar to Shadow V and Marianne—forward cockpit)

NAME	OWNER	DESIGNER/BLDR	DIMENSIONS	ENGINE	SPEED	SOURCE
ALTONIA II	Art Newby Miami, FL	Purdy Boat Co. Miami Beach, FL 1922	72′ × 14′ × 3′	2 V-12 Allisons	n/a	Y 11-'71 L '25

(Ran in Miami to Havana race; put in at Key West in rough conditions)

NAME	OWNER	DESIGNER/BLDR	DIMENSIONS	ENGINE	SPEED	SOURCE
ALSU Speedway Casco II	Paul Nelson W. Underhill New York, NY	Consolidated Morris Heights, NY 1917	78′ × 14′ × 5′	2 Speedways 2 GM 6-71s	n/a	Lloyds '31, '62
APHRODITE III Moonfire	John Pannell Pt. Washington, NY	Purdy Boat Co. Pt. Washington, NY 1937	74′ × 14′6″ × 3′5″ Hull #203	2 350-hp V8 Crusaders	25 knots	J Pannell CPM files A&C Bt. #8

(First set of engines—twin 800-hp V12 Packards—Model 3A-2500-Capitol conversions
1942 2d set of engines—twin 1350-hp V12 Packards—same model, 38 mph
1946-47 3d set of engines—twin 1500-hp V12 Packards—same model, 45 knots
1958 4th set of engines—twin 275-hp Hall-Scott Invaders, 26 knots
1969-70 5th set of engines—twin 275-hp 8V-81s GMs until 1978)

NAME	OWNER	DESIGNER/BLDR	DIMENSIONS	ENGINE	SPEED	SOURCE
APHRODITE II R-33567F	Jock Whitney Gif Warner n/a	Albany Boat Co. Albany, NY 1928	72′ × 14′ × 3′	2 V12 Wright Typhoons	32 knots	Lloyds '36 Y 5-'81

(At Blount Marine till '38 hurricane; abandoned at Essex, CT, some time before 1960)

NAME	OWNER	DESIGNER/BLDR	DIMENSIONS	ENGINE	SPEED	SOURCE
ARGO	H.P. Davidson n/a	John Wells/F.S. Nock East Greenwich, RI 1926	60′ × 12′6″ × 3′	2 Sterling Dolphins	n/a	Mystic Log '87 R 1-'27 P
ALLEZ Artmeis Florance	Robert LaVallee J.C. Faureau n/a	Chris Craft Algonac, MI 1929	48′ × 11′6″ Hull #6000	2 V8 454s-'91 2 V8 318s (older) 2 Chris Craft V8s	n/a	LaVallee files Y 4-'30 R, 2-'90

(Five of these 48′ stock commuters were built; this one was built in 1929 for Amy Guest of NY)

NAME	OWNER	DESIGNER/BLDR	DIMENSIONS	ENGINE	SPEED	SOURCE
ARDEA Governor's Lady	B.A. Dario State of MD	Consolidated Morris Heights, NY 1926	81′ × 11′ × 3′	2 Wright Typhoons Typhoons	n/a n/a	Lloyds '62 Briggs Ltr 4-'90

(Similar to *Nashira* and *Zingazee*, fast Consolidated houseboats, of which four or five were built; this one was once the Maryland Governor's official yacht)

NAME	OWNER	DESIGNER/BLDR	DIMENSIONS	ENGINE	SPEED	SOURCE
ARROW	Charles R. Flint Eli F. Whitney n/a	C.D. Mosher/ Samuel Ayers & Sons Nyack, NY 1900	132′ × 12′6″ × 3′6″	Steam Turbines 7000 hp	40.6 pmh	Steam Yts Power Boat

(One of the fastest cruisers ever built, timed over a measured mile on the Hudson River at 40.6 pmh in 1901; had many famous owners and was well used until the 1920s for commuting service)

NAME	OWNER	DESIGNER/BLDR	DIMENSIONS	ENGINE	SPEED	SOURCE
ANNABAR	James Cox n/a	Purdy/Consolidated Morris Heights, NY 1930	72′ × 14′ × 3′3″	2 Trieber Diesels	28 mph	Y5-'30, 11-'71
AMPHITRITE	J. Vanneck Glen Cove, NY	Robinson Seagull Benton Harbor, MI 1931	45′ × 10′ × 3′	2 Hall-Scotts	n/a	Lloyds '31
ANTICOSTI	Ray Schofield New York, NY	W. McInnis/ G. Lawley & Son Neponset, MA 1929	75′ × 13′9″ × 4′	2 6-cyl Wintons	n/a	NQ #17 P
ARROW	W. Stirgis San Diego, CA	Great Lakes Boatbuilding Milwaukee, WI 1923	54′ × 11′ × 2′6″	2 6-cyl Sterlings	n/a	Y 7-'23 P
AMARGO n/a	A. Cheesbrough	Luders Marine Stamford, CT 1916	36′ × 8′ × 2′6″	1 Van Blerck 30	n/a	Van Blerck catalog

(Jay Gould's *Atalanta*—1880s—commuter between Irvington and Manhattan—$75,000/year to run—54 officers and crew)

NAME	OWNER	DESIGNER/BLDR	DIMENSIONS	ENGINE	SPEED	SOURCE
ADIEU	Webb Jay Miami, FL, Chicago, IL	Purdy Boat Co. Trenton, MI 1923	46′ × 10′6″ × 2′10″	2 V12 Libertys	35 mph	MB Ad 1924 Lloyds '25
AVOCA	E.E. Dickinson, Jr. Essex, CT	Sparkman & Stephens/ Herreshoff Bristol, RI 1939	66′5″ × 13′6″ × 4′	2 500-hp V12 Kermaths	27 mph	Y 10-'32 P Lloyds '41
(H)ALL ALONE Helena	W. Pitt Dud Cates n/a	Consolidated Morris Heights, NY 1928	95′ × 16′ × 6′	2 Hall-Scotts 2 GM 6-110s	n/a	Lloyds '62 Lichenburg
ARIETE	J.I. Thornycroft England	Thornycroft's Chiswick, England 1887	147′ × 15′ × 6′	Steam	30 mph	Power Boat
AMERICANA	Ed Cutts Oxford, MD	Cutts & Case Oxford, MD 1992	65′ × 12′	1 Hall-Scott Invader	n/a	Cutts

(A replica commuter currently under construction using patented Ed Cutts method; many L. Francis Herreshoff ideas incorporated)

NAME	OWNER	DESIGNER/BLDR	DIMENSIONS	ENGINE	SPEED	SOURCE
AVOCETTE	Bob Tiedemann Newport, RI	Huckins Yacht Corp. #OS-48-20 Jacksonville, FL 1931	47′6″× 10′9″ × 3′	2 Sterling Petrels	n/a	CPM files
ALREMA	H. Leslie Atlass Chicago, IL	Henry C. Grebe/ Great Lakes Boatbuilding Milwaukee, WI 1932	74′8″ × 13′6″ × 3′6″	2 500-hp Wintons	30 mph	Y 3-'35 Lloyds '41
AVALON	J.A. Garland Buzzards Bay, MA	W. McInnis/Parkhurst Onset, MA 1926	36′11″ × 8′	1 V12 Liberty	40 mph	Lloyds '31
APPLEJACK	Paul Shields n/a	Luders Marine Stamford, CT 1927	72′ × 13′	2 Sterlings	27 mph	Y 8-'36

ALICIA—184′ Commodore John H. (?) Flagler (American Y.C.)

ADROIT 100′ steamer built by Consolidated in 1902 for A.G. Vanderbilt. Kept by Vanderbilt until 1908 when he bought Peter Rouss's first *Winchester*.

ALERT a patrol-boat type built in 1920 by the Herreshoffs for Charles A. Stone of Boston (and described as a commuter in *Herreshoff at Bristol*)—140′ × 138′ × 17′3″ × 6′4″—She was the last steam-powered vessel built by the Herreshoff yard.

NAME	OWNER	DESIGNER/BLDR	DIMENSIONS	ENGINE	SPEED	SOURCE
BALLYMENA—early Herreshoff high-speed steamer						
BIDGEE	n/a	Consolidated Morris Heights, NY 1928	n/a	2 Speedways	n/a	Mystic Log '87
BINK Wasp Paratus	M. Robinson La Belle, FL	John Wells/ Julius Peterson City Island, NY 1941	76′ × 18′7″ × 4′	3 GM 6-110s orig: 3-CurtisCon	n/a	Lloyds '67
	(Possibly used as a target boat in the Bay of Pigs Invasion. 1990: used in the movie "Havana." Now in West Indies.)					
BLACK CAESAR	Bob Collins Miami, FL	Forest Johnson Miami, FL 1957	32′ × 10′	2 Cadillac V8s 1 275-hp Crusader	n/a	Prowler '59 CPM Files
BAMBOLINA R #42604F	Theodore Pratt Glen Cove, NY	Luders Marine Hull #337 Stamford, CT 1929	46′ × 10′	2 6-cyl Kermaths	n/a	Y 11-'30 R 11-'30 Lloyds '31
BOOMERANG	n/a	W. Hand/Consolidated Morris Heights, NY 1916	37′ × 8′6″	1 8-cyl Van Blerck	n/a	Van Blerck catalog
BROOK II	P.R. Pyne II Roslyn, NY New York, NY	Tams & King/Peterson Nyack, NY 1926	57′6″ × 10′6″ × 3″	2 6-cyl 470-hp Sterlings	25 mph	R 6-'26 P R 12-'26 R Lloyds '31
	(Averaged more than 60 miles/day commuting)					
BONITO III	H. Bonbright n/a	W. McInnis/Lamb Squantum, ME 1930	55′6″ × 12′6″	2 6-cyl 235-hp Sterlings	n/a	Y 5-'31 Sterl. Ad
BLACK WATCH	Salvy Cofiero Brooklyn, NY	Tams, Lemoine & Crane/ NYYL&E Morris Heights, NY 1917	55′ × 11′4″ × 3′	1 Duesenberg	n/a	Lloyds '31 Mystic
BENGAL Topsal	Monahan (Dom Pizza) A.D. Wellman, Jr. n/a	Luders Marine Stamford, CT 1947	82′ × 16′	4 GM 6-110s	n/a	Lloyds '62
	(Seen in Fernandina Beach, FL, 11-'90; now a $90/night bed & breakfast)					

NAME	OWNER	DESIGNER/BLDR	DIMENSIONS	ENGINE	SPEED	SOURCE
BOSS	A.D. Goldman Charlevoix, MI	Lindsay Lord/ Great Lakes Boatbuilding Milwaukee, WI 1921	42' × 9'6" × 3'	1 Sterling	n/a	Don A. Hagerty 10-'90 Lloyds'31
BOXER	John I. Thornycroft England	Thornycroft's Chiswick, England 1895	180'	Steam	33.75 mph	Power Boat
	(First use of goggles aboard a fast boat)					
BETTY M IV	n/a	Consolidated Morris Heights, NY 1926	62' × 12' × 3'	2 6-cyl Speedways	n/a	Y 9-'28 Wells Ad
BONITA	Herm Oelrichs Greenport, NY	A. Loring Swasey/ G. Lawley & Son Neponset, MA 1917	63' × 13'	2 8-cyl Duesen- bergs	n/a	MB 7-'17 Ros #38628
BERANIA	Betty Carstairs England	Fred Cooper-Carstairs England 1932	57'6" × 12'6" × 2'3"	2 500-hp Napier Lions	31.8 knots	Y 4-'35 Uffa Fox II
	(Commuted between the owner's island, Whale Key, in the Bahamas and Miami)					
BLACK BIRD	Albert L. Smith Philadelphia, PA	Cox & Stevens/ Julius Peterson Nyack, NY 1928	94' × 14'	2 350-hp Wintons	21 mph	Y 11-'28
BOOMERANG II	Huston Wyeth NY	Swasey, Raymond & Page/Robert Jacob City Island, NY 1916	53' × 10' × 3'	2 12-cyl Van Blercks	32 mph	V Blrk Levic
BETTY M II	Com C. Kotcher Detroit, MI, Miami, FL	Carlton Wilby/ Church Boat n/a 1916	60' × 10' × 2'8"	2 Van Blercks	n/a	Van Blerck catalog
	(Won Detroit express-cruiser race in 1916)					
BOBCAT	Bradford Ellsworth Brooklyn, NY	Luders Marine Stamford, CT 1926	42' × 9' × 3'6"	1 Sterling	n/a	Lloyds '31
CABRILLA	August Heckscher Huntington, NY	William Atkin/ Atkin-Wheeler Huntington, NY 1914	115' × 12'6" × 3'	2 V8 750-hp	30 mph	NQ #17 Farmer, p 51

NAME	OWNER	DESIGNER/BLDR	DIMENSIONS	ENGINE	SPEED	SOURCE
	(A displacement-hull commuter with a corset stern; powered by custom engines, 5500 lbs each, 8″ bore × 13″ stroke with gasoline lines 1″ in diameter; engines designed by Bill Atkin, built by Cot Wheeler; wood imported from Russia; built in 9 months)					
CAMILLA	Matthew C.D. Borden Atlantic Highlands, NJ	Herreshoff Mfg. Co. Bristol, RI 1881	60′ × 9′ × 3′	Steam	18 mph	NQ #17
	(One of the first NYC commuters, built for Dr. H.C. Holrand)					
CATAMOUNT R# 39176FA	Brad Ellsworth Brooklyn, NY	Luders Marine Stamford, CT 1930	85′ × 15′ × 3′8″	2 1000-hp Wintons	27 mph	Y 2-, 3-'30
CATHALENE	C. Crane Newport, RI	Alden/Goudy & Stevens East Boothbay, ME 1929	38′ × 2′9″	2 6-cyl Sterlings	33 knots	Y 11-'30
CARRYALL	W.L. Mellon New York, NY	Purdy Boat Co. Port Washington, NY 1938	40′ × 10′3″ × 2′6″ Hull #210	2 6-cyl 150-hp Scripps	30 mph	Y 11-'70 Haney Purdy list
	(Last Purdy commuter built)					
CASSIAR Sea Hunter	Lt. Gen. K. Mellon Woods Hole, MA	B.T. Dobson/ Palmer Scott New Bedford, MA 1949	64′ × 15′ × 3′9″	2 GM 12-71s 960 hp '63	19 knots	Lloyds '62 Y '50 CPM files
	(Built mainly as a tuna fishing boat, but used by Mellon to commute occasionally)					
CHRISTINA Stormont	Aristotle Onassis Mediterranean	Vickers Montreal, Canada 1943	325′ × 36′6″ × 15′	2 triple-expansion steam engines	21 knots	CPM files
	(Built as escort frigate for Canadian Navy, converted to a yacht by Onassis after the war in Germany; with swimming pool, 8 deck boats, etc.; nothing like a commuter, but used for business and business travel; ran aground a few years ago coming into the Palm Beach inlet)					
CHARMING POLLY Joan (R#18472F) Owyhee	Col. H.H. Rogers New York, NY V.C. Moore Miami Beach, FL	F. Lurssen-Maybach Germany 1926	76′ × 13′6″	3 1350-hp Maybach Zeppelins	34.5 mph	MB 1-'26 R '26 (R) R 6-'27 Plan Y 7-'26 P
	(Well-known commuter, originally with three Maybach Zeppelin engines, later with twin 6-cyl Scripps)					
CIGARETTE Pocantino	W.H. Ames 1905-17 Barron Collier New York, NY	Swazey/G. Lawley & Son Neponset, MA 1905	126′ × 14′6″ × 4′5″	Steam	22 knots	Steam Yts
	(Probably the first Cigarette—100′ of length; devoted to propulsion machinery and crew)					

NAME	OWNER	DESIGNER/BLDR	DIMENSIONS	ENGINE	SPEED	SOURCE
CIGARETTE	L.G. Hamersley J. Doyla New York, NY	W. Hand/ Robert Jacob City Island, NY 1919	55' × 9'10"	2 800-hp Murray & Tregurthas 1923: 2 Libertys	38 mph	WB #28 R 7-'25 Lloyds '25

(First of Gordon Hamersley's Cigarettes, a 38-mph commuter that beat the NY Central Train to Albany)

NAME	OWNER	DESIGNER/BLDR	DIMENSIONS	ENGINE	SPEED	SOURCE
CIGARETTE	n/a	W. Hand/n/a n/a 1923	40' × 10' × 3'	2 Murray & Tregurthas 35 mph	35 mph	R '24

(Last of Hand's express power boats; possibly owned by L.G. Hamersley)

| CIGARETTE
Gar Sr.
R #1044F,
10120F | L.G. Hamersley
G. Wood
Don Ault
New York, NY | Gar Wood
Algonac, MI
1923 | 70' × 11'6" × 3' | 5 450-hp V12
Libertys | 50 mph | MB 11-'26
NQ #17
Lloyds '25 |

(Currently afloat in Mt. Clemens, MI, raised from a sinking; with 5 Libertys used 2 1000-gal gas tanks; now has 2 8-cyl Packard flatheads; being restored by John and George Malkovitch)

| CIGARETTE
Nepenthe
Philijean | L.G. Hamersley
Steve Hammer
6-'89
n/a | John Wells/Nevins
City Island, NY
1928 | 75' × 12'11" × 4' | 2 6-cyl Wintons | 29 mph | R 11-'28,
11-'27
Y 7-'28 |

(Similar to *Cossack*, *Frolic II*)

| CHEBOYGAN | J.F. Reiss
NY | Gar Wood
Algonac, MI
1931 | 40' × 10' × 2'6" | 2 200-hp Scripps | 34 mph | Y 4-'31
Scripps ad |

| CHRIS II | Fred Crispin
Philadelphia, PA | L.C.
Wilmington, DE
1927 | 58' × 11' | 2 550-hp
Hall-Scotts | n/a | Crispin |

| CORISANDE
R #10263F | Marshall Field
Chicago, IL | Gar Wood/Nevins
NY
1923 | 50' × 10'3" × 4' | 2 V12 Libertys
2 Wright Typhoons | n/a | Mot Yat 1-'88 |

(Well-known commuter, captained by John Stafford for many years; Typhoons installed in 1925)

| COSSACK | G.W. Moffett
New York, NY,
Greenwich, CT | John Wells/Consolidated
Morris Heights, NY
1930 | 75'6" × 13' × 4' | 2 8-cyl Wintons | n/a | MB 1-'35
Lloyds '31 |

(Similar to *Jessica*, *Frolic*, *Sazarac II*)

| CONEJO | G.W. Raine
New York, NY | Consolidated
Morris Heights, NY
1922 | 91'6" × 14' | 2 8-cyl Sterlings | 30 mph | Y 10-'82
R 5-'22 |

NAME	OWNER	DESIGNER/BLDR	DIMENSIONS	ENGINE	SPEED	SOURCE
CRIMPER Sea Hawk	J.S. Cosden Palm Beach, FL	Consolidated Morris Heights, NY 1923	60' × 9'6" × 3'	2 6-cyl 600-hp Speedways	30 mph	Y, R 12-'23
CYRIC Wayfarer	Robert Morse Boston, MA	G. Lawley & Son Neponset, MA 1926	68' × 12'5" × 3'8"	2 Sterling Dolphins 1948: 2 GM 6-71s	n/a	Y 10-'27 Lloyds '62
CHEROKEE	Malcolm Brown Norwich, CT	Consolidated Morris Heights, NY 1924	45' × 11'6" × 3'	2 V8 Palmers	n/a	Brown
		(Formerly owned by Heinz family, Drayton Cochran, Alexander Smith carpet family; seen at 1989 Mystic Seaport Antique Boat Show)				
COUNTESS (R #354f&e)	W. Hand H.P. Scott Long Island, NY	W. Hand/ G. Lawley & Son Neponset, MA 1916	39'4" × 9'5"	1 8-cyl ??	n/a	MB 8-'16,10-'16 R '24 Lloyds '25
		(William Hand's first V-bottom express cruiser; established record on Hudson and Long Island Sound; terrorized contemporary express cruisers at speed)				
COUNTESS	L.G. Hamersley Long Island, NY	Ford & Paine/Jacobs City Island, NY 1925	55' × 14' × 3'	1 6-cyl Scripps	n/a	Lloyds '25
COQUETTE	L.B. Moore New York, NY	Consolidated Morris Heights, NY 1926	58' × 14' × 4'	2 6-cyl Speedways	n/a	R 8-'26
CORISANDE II Valkerise	S.L. Slover Marshall Field Lloyds Neck, NY	Purdy Boat Co. Port Washington, NY 1932	65' × 13'8"	2 12-cyl Hall-Scotts	n/a	Mot Yat 1-'88 Lloyds '41
CLOVER	n/a	Herreshoff Mfg. Co. Bristol, RI 1901	81' × 15'	1 Herreshoff triple-expansion steam engine	n/a	Yts 1000ls Lloyds '07
CORAS III	Ken G. Smith Chicago, IL	Henry C. Grebe/ Great Lakes Boatbuilding Milwaukee, WI 1931	n/a	2 Sterlings	n/a	R 5-'31
CANVASBACK Zara	Fred Hard Greenwich, CT	Herreshoff Mfg. Co. Bristol, RI 1909	59'8" × 10'7" × 3'	1 Steam 1 V8 Palmer	n/a	Lloyds '62 Hard
		(This vintage Herreshoff commuter is currently at the Philadelphia Maritime Museum)				

NAME	OWNER	DESIGNER/BLDR	DIMENSIONS	ENGINE	SPEED	SOURCE
COSSACK	Galen Stone Boston, MA	G. Lawley & Son Neponset, MA 1916	64' × 9'6" × 3'	2 Van Blercks	n/a	Van Blerck catalog
CORSAIR Corsair (I) Kanapha	C.J. Osborn J.P. Morgan (1982-90) n/a	W. Cramp & Sons Philadelphia, PA 1880	185' × 23'7" × 10'	Steam	n/a	Steam Yts

(The first of the Morgan *Corsairs*, built for C.J. Osborne, acquired by J.P. Morgan in 1881)

NAME	OWNER	DESIGNER/BLDR	DIMENSIONS	ENGINE	SPEED	SOURCE
CORSAIR (II)	J.P. Morgan New York, NY	J. Beavor-Webb/ Neafie & Levy n/a 1890	241'6" × 27' × 13'	Steam 2000 hp	17 knots	Steam Yts

(Morgan used this beautiful yacht nearly as much as he used various homes; she was Flagship of the NYYC and always the lead boat in the club's cruises; served well except for single screw)

NAME	OWNER	DESIGNER/BLDR	DIMENSIONS	ENGINE	SPEED	SOURCE
CORSAIR (III)	J.P. Morgan New York, NY	J. Beavor-Webb/ T.S. Marvel Newburgh, NY 1899	304' × 33'6" × 16'	2 triple-expansion steam engines 6000 hp	19 knots	Steam Yts

(Considered by many astute yachtsmen to be the finest motor yacht ever built, known worldwide for her almost perfect proportions, speed, and seaworthiness; she was the most beloved of J. Pierpont Morgan's many possessions and saw 45 years of rigorous service not only as a yacht but during two World Wars)

NAME	OWNER	DESIGNER/BLDR	DIMENSIONS	ENGINE	SPEED	SOURCE
CORSAIR (IV) R #69354F	J.P. "Jack" Morgan New York, NY	H. Gielow/ Bath Iron Works Bath, ME 1930	343'6" × 42'7" × 18'	2 GE turbo electric engines	n/a	Steam Yts

(Said to be the most nearly perfect large yacht ever constructed; this last and largest *Corsair* was a familiar sign during East Coast yachting events in the 1930s, and served Jack Morgan as a sometime commuter. Note: Morgan's yachts were not numbered; the R number is used here only as a reference)

NAME	OWNER	DESIGNER/BLDR	DIMENSIONS	ENGINE	SPEED	SOURCE
CORSAIR (Deck Boat)	Jim Lewis Clayton, NY	Herreshoff Mfg. Co. Bristol, RI 1930	35' × 8' × 3'	1 V8 Chevrolet	30 mph	CPM files Lewis

(All that is left of the mighty Corsairs; seen at many ACBS shows; all teak)

NAME	OWNER	DESIGNER/BLDR	DIMENSIONS	ENGINE	SPEED	SOURCE
COMET	Sidney Ehrman CA	John Hacker/ Fellows & Stewart Wilmington, CA 1922	36' × 8' × 3'	Scripps	n/a	CPM files
COMET II	H.L. Williams Miami, FL	E.D. Purdy/ G. Lawley & Son Neponset, MA 1920	36'7" × 9'8" × 2'10"	1 Speedway	n/a	Lloyds '28

NAME	OWNER	DESIGNER/BLDR	DIMENSIONS	ENGINE	SPEED	SOURCE
DAISY—early Herreshoff "flyer"?						
DARK ISLAND	F.G. Bourne New York, NY, Thousand Islands	Seabury/Gas Eng & Power Morris Heights, NY 1912	60′ × 10′6″ × 3′	1 6-cyl Speedway	20 knots	Lloyds '25 1000 Isle Yts
(This was the first of Consolidated's Speedway series of commuters; originally a day boat and island commuter; in the 1940s she went to Florida and was used until the 1960s under the name *Roberic*)						
DOLPHIN	J. Simard Montreal, Canada	Consolidated Morris Heights, NY 1929	66′ × 12′6″ × 3′3″	2 6-cyl Speedways	n/a	Lloyds '62 Clayton '89
(Similar to *Mohican, Ragtime*, other Speedway commuters; same captain for 45 years and same owners since built; came to ACBS commuter show at Clayton, NY, 1989)						
DORICA R #33180F	Chas. N. Edge Rye, NY	F. Luerssen Germany 1928	47′ × 12′ × 4′	2 600-hp V12 Maybachs	30 mph	NQ #21 Y 10-, 12-'28
(One of the Luerssen express yachts sold by Maybach in New York, NY; commuted from Rye to Manhattan)						
DAUNTLESS R #147493F	Lawrance Rockefellar Hudson, NY	Sparkman & Stephens/ Jakobson Shipyard Oyster Bay, NY 1949	65′10″ × 17′6″ × 3′	2 4M-2500 V12 Packards	41 knots	NQ #17 Lloyds '62 Y 10-'82
(Impressive later Hudson River commuter still in use)						
DOG STAR	F.D. Allen Providence, RI	W. Hand/F.S. Nock E. Greenwich, RI 1922	40′ × 9′6″ × 3′	2 6-cyl Sterlings	24 mph	Y 12-'22
DONMARGO	C.E. Breen LI Sound, NY	Consolidated Morris Heights, NY 1930	81′ × 15′ × 4′	2 500-hp Wintons	20 mph	R 5-'31, 9-'30 Y 9-'30 Briggs
(Being restored in Boston, MA)						
DAWN	T.H. Newbury n/a	Herreshoff Mfg. Co. Bristol, RI 1912	81′ × 15′	Steam	n/a	NQ #17
DISPATCH R #40438F	Herreshoff n/a	Herreshoff/Britt Bros. MA 1927	46′9″ × 9′5″	2 180—hp Hispano Suizas	28 mph	Y 3-'28 LFH Ad
DOLPHIN	A.G. Milbank Huntington, NY	T.D. Bowes/Dauntless Essex, CT 1925	55′ × 12′ × 3′	2 6-cyl Gar Woods	n/a	Lloyds '31

NAME	OWNER	DESIGNER/BLDR	DIMENSIONS	ENGINE	SPEED	SOURCE
DODGER III	H.L. Pratt Glen Cove, NY	Consolidated Morris Heights, NY 1920	60′ × 11′ × 3′8″	2 8-cyl Sterlings	20 mph	Lloyds '25
DELIGHT	R. Arthur Fulton Huntington, NY	F.D. Lawley Neponsit, MA 1918	62′ × 12′ × 4′	2 8-cyl Speedways	21 mph	Lloyds '31
ELDA	Arthur V. Davis Miami, FL	Krogerwerft Germany 1954	52′ × 14′ × 4′	2 Mercedes V8s 1958	32 mph	Lloyds '62
EDAMENA II	E.P. Carlton Fall River, MA	W. Hand/ G. Lawley & Son Neponset, MA 1916	45′ × 9′6″ × 3′	2 6-cyl Van Blercks	25 mph	Van Blerck catalog
ELEGANT LADY	D. McAllen Bradenton, FL (Destroyed 1987)	Consolidated Morris Heights, NY 1929	65′ × 13′ × 3′6″	2 GM 6-71s	n/a	CPM files
EARLY BIRD	W. Ryle New York, NY	Consolidated Morris Heights, NY 1920	55′ × 8′6″ × 2′10″	2 6-cyl Speedways	n/a	Lloyds '28, '31
ERYHOME	Robert C. Ream Stamford, CT	W. McInnis/ G. Lawley & Son Neponset, MA 1930	75′ × 14′3″ × 3′1″	2 6-cyl Wintons	n/a	WBt #52 Lloyds '31
ESPERANCE	H.W. Schneider Bowness, England	T.B. Seath Clydeside, Scotland 1869	65′ × 10′ × 4′	1 Steam V-eng 2 screws	n/a	CPM files Gt Age Steam

(Oldest known boat built as commuter and marked the start of commuting by powerboat; owned by George H. Pattinson of the Windermere Steamboat Museum and still in use on Lake Windermere)

NAME	OWNER	DESIGNER/BLDR	DIMENSIONS	ENGINE	SPEED	SOURCE
EXCALIBUR Lady Babs	Barnard Lake Winnipesaukee, NH	Chris Craft Algonac, MI 1929	38′ × 9′9″ × 2′8″	1 Scripps V12	n/a	Ant Bt Mag Vol II #2

(One of the 16 Chris Craft 38′ commuters in use at ACBS boat shows. Model #122, 62 built by Chris Craft)

NAME	OWNER	DESIGNER/BLDR	DIMENSIONS	ENGINE	SPEED	SOURCE
EPEE R #33592F	Ed. E. Plant New York, NY	Luders Marine Stamford, CT 1929	58′ × 11′9″ × 3′8″	2 6-cyl 600-hp Sterlings	25 mph	R 7-'29

NAME	OWNER	DESIGNER/BLDR	DIMENSIONS	ENGINE	SPEED	SOURCE
ELIZABETH ANN III	Mrs. Charles Kelley NY	NYYL&E Co. Morris Heights, NY 1930	75′ × 15′6″ × 3′3″	2 6-cyl Twentieth Centurys	n/a	Briggs Lloyds '31
ESCAPADE Sea Gull	n/a	Consolidated Morris Heights, NY 1925	61′ × 12′6″ × 4′	2 GM 6-71s	n/a	CPM files

(One of Consolidated's Speedway series; ended her days supposedly in Florida in the 1960s)

ESTELLE—early (1877) Hereshoff flyer—16 mph—used as Cuban gunrunner, later as New Orleans tugboat (?)

NAME	OWNER	DESIGNER/BLDR	DIMENSIONS	ENGINE	SPEED	SOURCE
ELLIDE	R. Warren Philadelphia, PA	C.D. Moshers/S. Ayers Nyack, NY 1896	81′ × 8′4″ × 3′2″	1 910-hp Steam	34 knots	Stm Yachts

(Well-known fast flyer—clocked at 34 knots)

NAME	OWNER	DESIGNER/BLDR	DIMENSIONS	ENGINE	SPEED	SOURCE
FRIENDSHIP	Mirick Friend Newton, MA	Chris Craft #5050 Algonac, MI 1929	38′ × 9′9″ × 2′8″	1 350-hp Chrysler V8	n/a	CPM files ACBS
FROLIC	Walter P. Chrysler New York, NY	Consolidated Morris Heights, NY 1923	62′ × 12′ × 3′4″	2 6-cyl Speedways	n/a	Lloyds '25
FROLIC II	Walter P. Chrysler New York, NY	John Wells/ G. Lawley & Son Neponset, MA 1925	70′ × 12′6″	2 6-cyl Wintons	n/a	Lloyds '25
FROLIC III R #16673F	Walter P. Chrysler New York, NY	John Wells/Mathis Camden, NJ 1928	75′ × 13′ × 3′11″	2 8-cyl Wintons	30 mph	R 11-'28 MB 1-'35

(Similar to *Cigarette II, Jessica;* commuted between Kings Point and Manhattan)

NAME	OWNER	DESIGNER/BLDR	DIMENSIONS	ENGINE	SPEED	SOURCE
FILLETTE	J.W. Kiser Glen Cove, NY	Consolidated Morris Heights, NY 1920	80′ × 13′6″	2 Speedways	n/a	R 1-'30 My Lg '87
FIGGET	H.S. Vanderbilt LI Sound, NY	Purdy Boat Co. Port Washington, NY 1930	35′ × 8′ × 3′	2 Scripps	45 mph	R 1-'30

(Runabout commuter used on Long Island Sound by Vanderbilts)

NAME	OWNER	DESIGNER/BLDR	DIMENSIONS	ENGINE	SPEED	SOURCE
FRANCIS	J.H. Dodge Detroit, MI	Great Lakes Boatbuilding Milwaukee 1923	104′ × 15′ × 4′	4 Murray & Tregurthas	31.3 mph	R 1-'21 R 5-'22

NAME	OWNER	DESIGNER/BLDR	DIMENSIONS	ENGINE	SPEED	SOURCE
FEVRIER	Mrs. St. George Great Britain	Vosper England 1935	45′ × 9′	2 Sterlings	n/a	YTG 10-'35
		(Used as commuter in 1930s between Isle of Wight and England's South Coast on almost daily basis)				
FLYER	B.H. Borden New York, NY	Consolidated Morris Heights, NY 1914	66′ × 10′6″ × 3′	2 6-cyl Sterlings	27 mph	R 6-'14, 3-'17
		(Commuted between Red Bank, NJ and Manhattan)				
GAR JR.	Gar Wood n/a	Gar Wood/Chris Smith Algonac, MI 1921	50′ × 9′ × 2′10″	2 900-hp V12 Libertys	40+ mph	MB 12-'26 R 5-'22
		(First of Gar Wood's commuter-style cruisers built by Chris Smith)				
GAR SR. Cigarette R #20629F	Gar Wood L.G. Hamersley n/a	Gar Wood Algonac, MI 1923	70′ × 11′6″ × 4′6″	4 V12 Libertys 2 V12 Allisons	n/a	Lloyds '62-'67 CPM files
		(Famous commuter, now used as houseboat in Mt. Clemens, MI, engines out; see *Cigarette*)				
GAR JR. II Corisande	Gar Wood Marshall Field n/a	Gar Wood/Nevins City Island, NY 1923	50′ × 10′3″ × 4′	2 450-hp V12 Smith-built Libertys	n/a	R 2-'23 Y 6-, 7-'22
		(As Gar Jr., raced from Miami to Havana—240 miles in 9 hr., 23 min.; later became Marshall Field's *Corisande*; twin 650-hp Wright Typhoons installed in 1925)				
GAR SR. II	G.H. Hamersley Oyster Bay, NY	Gar Wood Algonac, MI 1927	50′ × 12′8″	2 450-hp V12 Gar Wood Libertys	n/a	R 6-'27 Y 9-'30
GODDESS Empress	Richard duPont Wilmington, DE	Consolidated Morris Heights, NY 1947	58′ × 14′ × 3′6″	2 GM 6-71s	18 knots	Llloyds '62
		(For sale since 1992)				
GREYHOUND Get There R #929S	Edsel Ford E.L. Richards n/a	Tams, Lemoine & Crane/ Wood & McClure City Island, NY 1916	58′6″ × 10′5″ × 4′	2 Van Blercks, replaced in 1927 by 2 V12 Packards	n/a	MB 1-'26 Lloyds '28
GREY GULL	W.S. Carpenter Wilmington, DE	Consolidated Morris Heights, NY 1934	66′6″ × 14′4″ × 4′	2 600-hp Speedways	23 mph	R 11-'34 Y 2-'35
GEM	Will Ziegler New York, NY	Maybach-F. Luerssen Germany 1930	102′ × 17′ × 4′6″	3 V12 Maybachs 1650 hp	28 mph	Y 10-'28, 2-'30

NAME	OWNER	DESIGNER/BLDR	DIMENSIONS	ENGINE	SPEED	SOURCE
GEREDNA R #42480F	J.H. Higgins n/a	Luders Marine Stamford, CT 1930	72′ × 13′6″ × 3′9″	2 8-cyl Sterling Dolphins	n/a	Y, R 11-'30 Lloyds '31
GRAYLING IV	O.J. Mulford Detroit, MI	Gidley Boat Works Ontario, Canada 1926	32′ × 10′8″ × 3′	2 360-hp 6-cyl Grays	n/a	R 11-'26
GO GO	n/a Pt. Washington, NY	Consolidated Morris Heights, NY 1923	64′ × 13′ × 3′	2 6-cyl Speedways	n/a	Y 2-'89 Fexas
GEM Condor	H.P. vanKnauf New York, NY	Cox & Stevens/ G. Lawley & Son Neponset, MA 1913	164′ × 19′ × 4′6″	2 Steam	n/a	Steam Yt

(Used as commuter on Long Island Sound; served as petrol vessel in World Wars I and II)

NAME	OWNER	DESIGNER/BLDR	DIMENSIONS	ENGINE	SPEED	SOURCE
HALLIE R	C.A. Bennett Kansas City, MO	Chris Craft Algonac, MI 1929	38′ × 9′9″ × 2′8″	1 Chris Craft	30 mph	R 4-'31
HARPOON II	P. Nicholson Providence, RI	G. Lawley & Son Neponset, MA 1923	68′ × 12′6″	2 6-cyl Sterlings	22 mph	R 1-'23
HARMATTAN R #29677F	J.N. Ottley New York, NY	F.P. Humphrys/ Roland Werft Germany 1928	49′ × 11′ × 3′	2 6-cyl Sterlings	n/a	Lloyds '28, '31, 41
HALL BY HERSELF Shadow J R #75138F	N. Andrews New York, NY	Purdy Boat Co. Trenton, MI 1924	56′ × 11′7′ × 3′	2 6-cyl Hall-Scotts	n/a	Y 8-'36 Lloyds '41
HARBEL	Harvey Firestone	Robinson Marine Benton Harbor, MI 1933	48′ × 11′ × 3′4″	2 Scripps	n/a	R 3-'34
HAWK	G.J. Ottley Locust Valley, NY	Consolidated Morris Heights, NY 1933	47′ × 10′ × 3′	2 250-hp Speedways	30 mph	R 10-'33, 9-'34
HIGH STRUNG	Rum Boat Sakonnet, NJ	Herreshoff Mfg. Co. Bristol, RI	45′	1 Liberty	n/a	Rum Wars

NAME	OWNER	DESIGNER/BLDR	DIMENSIONS	ENGINE	SPEED	SOURCE
HELENA R #28279F	C.E.F. McCann New York, NY	Consolidated Morris Heights, NY 1928	95′ × 16′ × 4′8″	2 8-cyl Speedways	n/a	R 11-'28
HIAWATHA	J.B. Ford Detroit, MI	Consolidated Morris Heights, NY 1924	85′ × 15′ × 3′6″	2 300-hp Speedways	22 mph	R 4-'25
HOOSIER V	H.R. Duckwall Indianapolis, IN Miami, FL	F. Lawley/ G. Lawley & Son Neponset, MA 1920	42′ × 9′11″ × 2′6″	2 6-cyl Sterlings	31 mph	R 4-'20
HURRY UP II	C.G. Conway NY	W. Hand Fairhaven, MA 1922	65′ × 12′6″ × 3′	2 6-cyl Sterlings	29 mph	R 2-'27, 11-'38 Lloyds '28
INDOLENT	S.V.R. Cruger Oyster Bay, NY	n/a	68′	n/a	n/a	NQ #17
IOTA Lonestar R #40739F	H.W. Ingersoll Bridgeport, CT	Consolidated Morris Heights, NY 1920	52′ × 11′3″ × 2′9″	2 8-cyl Speedways	28 mph	R 7-'33 Lloyds '28
JADA	C. Harding Boston, MA	G. Lawley & Son Neponset, MA 1920	56′ × 11′3″ × 2′9″	2 6-cyl Sterlings	n/a	Lloyds '25
JEAN	T.A. Gillespie New York, NY	Herreshoff Mfg. Co. Bristol, RI 1897	77′6″ × 10′6″ × 5′	Steam	n/a	1000 Isles
JESSICA Jem	Ted Valpey Dover, NH	John Wells/Consolidated Morris Heights, NY 1930	75′6″ × 13′6″ × 4′	1947: 2 GM 6-110s	n/a	CPM files

(Built for Jeremiah Milbank, later owned by George Lauder; Captain Raymond Thombs with boat since the end of WWII; cruised to Canada with Commuters '89)

NAME	OWNER	DESIGNER/BLDR	DIMENSIONS	ENGINE	SPEED	SOURCE
JUDITH	R.R. Barney Balaban New London, CT	Robinson Marine Benton Harbor, MI 1935	56′ × 12′ × 4′	2 GM 6-71s	n/a	Lloyds '62 Speltz

(Perhaps the largest Robinson commuter; cost $60,000 to build; used by Paramount Pictures; now on the Chesapeake)

NAME	OWNER	DESIGNER/BLDR	DIMENSIONS	ENGINE	SPEED	SOURCE
JULIE M II Little Stranger Ragtime R #28976F	M.M. Smith n/a	Consolidated Morris Heights, NY 1928	64′ × 12′6″ × 3′	2 6-cyl Speedways	n/a	R 11-'28

(Completely rebuilt in Maine with new power)

NAME	OWNER	DESIGNER/BLDR	DIMENSIONS	ENGINE	SPEED	SOURCE
JOANEDA R #48858F	R.B. Anderson Boston, MA	Robinson Marine Benton Harbor, MI 1933	50′ × 11′3″ × 3′	2 6-cyl 275-hp Hall-Scotts	n/a	??
JAVELIN—early Herreshoff speed steamer or "flyer"			98′ × 104″ × 14′9″	2 3-cyl Steam	n/a	CPM files
JOLLY ROGER	Robert Drum n/a	Chris Craft Algonac, MI 1926	22′ × 6′10″ × 2′6″	1 6-cyl 75-hp Chrysler Ace	n/a	CPM files
(One of the smallest commuters in use; interesting history)						
KANAWHA	H.H. Rogers New York, NY	Bath Iron Works Bath, ME 1909	75′ × 13′11″ × 4′	2 6-cyl Steam Holmes	n/a	Lloyds '25 NQ #17
KATOURA Sly Mongoose	Robert Tod New York, NY	W. McInnis/ G. Lawley & Son Neponset, MA 1922	44′ × 10′4″ × 2′6″	2 6-cyl Speedways	n/a	WBT #52, 54 R 11-'22
(Owned by Drayton Cochran as Sly Mongoose; one mahogany log used in hull planking; served in WWII as Coast Guard patrol boat)						
KATHMAR III	R.T. Fowler Lenox, MA	Luders Marine Stamford, CT 1922	50′ × 9′9″ × 3′	2 6-cyl Sterlings	n/a	CPM files Lloyds '25
KEN ROSS	n/a	George Crouch/ Howard Lyon n/a 1931	42′ × 9′ × 2′6″	2 6-cyl Sterlings	n/a	R 2-'31
KINGFISHER	J.M. Goetchins n/a	W. Hand/ G. Lawley & Son Neponset, MA 1916	60′ × 10′ × 3′	2 6-cyl Van Blercks	n/a	Van Blerck catalog
KYRRAH	H.E. Noyes Boston, MA	G. Lawley & Son Neponset, MA 1927	55′ × 9′6″ × 3′	2 6-cyl 200-hp Hall-Scotts	n/a	R 3-'27
KATY FITZ	Kath Spaulding Detroit, MI	Consolidated Morris Heights, NY 1925	38′ × 7′ × 2′9″	1 6-cyl Chris Craft	n/a	??
KEGONSA	n/a	Consolidated Morris Heights, NY 1926	81′ × 14′6″ × 4′	2 V12 Wright Typhoons	28 mph	Briggs
(Similar to *Nashira*, one of the Consolidated fast houseboat commuters)						

NAME	OWNER	DESIGNER/BLDR	DIMENSIONS	ENGINE	SPEED	SOURCE
LUZ	n/a Columbia South America	Hickman Seasled Mystic, CT 1922	51' × 12' × 2'6"	2 6-cyl Sterling Dolphins	34 mph	Y 11-'22
LONE STAR	George Bourne Mrs. Harriman n/a	Consolidated Morris Heights, NY 1920	81' × 14'6" × 4'	2 V12 Wright Typhoons	28 mph	Y 1-'23 R 7-'33
	(Possibly first of the Consolidated houseboat fast commuters. Similar to *Nashira* and *Kegonsa*)					
LOTOWANA	H.H. Rogers LI Sound, NY	W. Hand n/a 1923	65' × 12'6' × 3'	2 600-hp 8-cyl Sterlings	26 mph	Y 1-'23
LIGHTNIN'	W. Wickwire Buffalo, NY	Ditchburn Gravenhurst, Ontario 1923	42' × 9'3' × 2'3'	2 Sterling Sea Gulls	n/a	Y 12-'23
LOTTY K R #30915F	Adolph Zukor New York, NY	Tams & King/ Julius Peterson Nyack, NY 1927	49' × 10' × 3'	2 V12 Packards 1100 hp	45 mph	Y 9-'27 R 11-'28
LURA M III R #19105F	W.A. Fisher Detroit, MI	John Wells/Consolidated Morris Heights, NY 1926	80' × 14' × 5'	2 6-cyl 700-hp Wintons	22 mph	Y 9-'27
LITTLE SOVERIGN	Matthew C.D. Borden Atlantic Highlands, NJ	Herreshoff Mfg. Co. Bristol, RI 1904	112' × 11'6"	2 Herreshoff triple-expansion steam engines	n/a	Yts 1000 Isl NQ #17
LAUGHING LADY	Mrs. Bradley R.D.L. Gardiner Gardiners Island, NY	Luders Marine Stamford, CT 1947	33'2" × 9'	2 Volvos	n/a	CPM files Lloyds '62, '75
	(Still in use as commuter to go to and from Gardiner's Island to Greeport, Long Island)					
LOCKPAT II	Dick Locke Dave Stevens Detroit, MI	John Hacker/ Hacker Boat Co. Mt. Clements, MI 1942	40' × 10'6"	2 650-hp V12 Packards	60 mph	SpdBt p 168
LANCER Phoenix Gloria	Ted Conover Ft. Lauderdale, FL Edward Bowes n/a	Sparkman & Stevens/ Consolidated Morris Heights, NY 1937	65'8" × 12' × 3'6"	1958: 2 GM 6-71s	n/a	Lloyds '62 CPM files
	(Built for Major Edward Bowes and much used as a commuter in Florida; sold in 1980s and trucked to San Diego, CA; beautiful boat, still in use; now called *Old Age*)					

NAME	OWNER	DESIGNER/BLDR	DIMENSIONS	ENGINE	SPEED	SOURCE
LOUISA	J.P. Morgan Cragston, NY	n/a 1872	n/a	Steam	n/a	Hs of Morg

(This steam launch is probably the first American commuter; took Morgan across the Hudson from his country home, Cragston, to the NY Central train station and then to Wall Street; Morgan became interested in commuters, leading to the mighty Corsairs)

LION'S WHELP	Phineas Shaw Sprague Palm Beach, FL	W. Hand/ Hodgdson Bros. East Boothbay, ME 1929	72' × 16'10"	2 6-cyl Hall-Scotts	n/a	WD BT #52 Lloyds '41

(First and most beautiful of the famous *Lion's Whelps,* lost in Broward yard fire in Ft. Lauderdale during the 1960s)

LUCKY STRIKE R #60745F	D.C. Hard New York, NY	Consolidated Morris Heights, NY 1931	55' × 12'	2 6-cyl Speedways	25 mph	R 7-'32
LINDA MAR	Ian Kennedy Canada	Chris Craft #5020 Algonac, MI 1929	38' × 9'6"	1 V8 Chris Craft	n/a	ACBS
LADY NINA	Chas. E. Proctor n/a	Purdy Boat Co. Port Washington, NY 1931	72' × 14' × 3'8" Hull #160	2 Treiblers	n/a	R 9-'31
LITTLE SOVERIGN II	Matthew C.D. Borden Atlantic Highlands, NJ	Consolidated Morris Heights, NY 1909	137' × 13'6" × 3'6"	2 triple-expansion steam engines	n/a	St Ycts NQ #17

(Was beaten by *Winchester II* in impromptu race, causing M.C.D. Borden to have larger, faster commuter designed and built by Consolidated)

LITTLE STRANGER Ragtime	Mrs. Fred Hard Greenwich, CT	Consolidated Morris Heights, NY 1928	64' × 12' × 3'6"	2 GM 6-71s	n/a	Lloyds '62, '67, '74 Y10-'40
LITTLE VIKING II R #22644F	George Baker New York, NY	Consolidated Morris Heights, NY 1927	70' × 12'6"	2 Speedways	27 mph	R 8-'27 Mct Lg

LOTUS SEEKER—1892 Herreshoff similar to *Clover, Scout, Stroller.* One of the few that ended up as a rumboat

MAKAIRA	Les Sears Palm Peach, FL	F. Geiger/Trumpy Annapolis, MD 1946	70' × 15'4" × 5'	1953: 2 GM 6-110s	n/a	Lloyds '62

NAME	OWNER	DESIGNER/BLDR	DIMENSIONS	ENGINE	SPEED	SOURCE
MARLIN R #70066F	D. Acierno Sayville, NY	W. McInnis/ G. Lawley & Son Neponset, MA 1930	51'6" × 12'5' × 3'	2 Sterling Dolphins Dolphins 2 V8 Chryslers	n/a	R 4-'31 WBT #52 Lloyds '62

(Well-known commuter built for Edsel Ford and later owned by the Kennedy family; one of five similar McInnis designs taken from *Bonito III, Pronto I & II, Lindale*; still in original shape; serves the Acierno family well during summers on Long Island Sound)

| MARIANNE
R #6319F | n/a | Purdy Boat Co.
Miami Beach, FL
1919 | 55' × 10'6" × 2'3"
Hull #23 | 2 Speedways | n/a | R 5-'23
Y 11-'71
Purdy list |

(Similar to Purdy commuters *Shadow V* and *Altonia*)

MARJO	Joe McAleenan New York, NY	Albany Boat Co. Watervliet, NY 1917	40' × 9'6"	1 8-cyl Duesenberg	36 mph	??
MARLEN V	W.T. Grant New York, NY	Consolidated Morris Heights, NY n/a	50'6" × 12'6" × 3'10"	2 Speedways	n/a	R. Stanny
MAXINE R #29132F	Tex Rickard New York, NY	John Wells/ G. Lawley & Son Neponset, MA 1928	70' × 12'6" × 3'6"	2 6-cyl Wintons	n/a	R 11-'28
MIKI JANE	A.R. Lowe Glen Cove, NY	John Hacker Mt. Clemens, MI 1930	38' × 8'6" × 3'	2 Sterlings	n/a	Lloyds '31 Sharpless
MOUSER	Senator George Harding Chicago, IL	P. Little/Ramaley Wayzata, MN 1916	43'9" × 7'6" × 28"	1 V12 Van Blerck	44 mph	R 9-'17 MB 8-'76
MIDNIGHT LACE	John North St. Michaels, MD	Tom Fexas/Lace Yachts Stuart, FL 1979	44' × 11' × 2'10"	2 6-cyl 210-hp Renaults	30 mph	CPM files

(Modern version of rumrunner-commuter; this was first of the type, built for Jim Lewis, now owned by Judge John C. North of St. Michaels, MD)

| MONATONA | Ed Noble
n/a | Ditchburn
Gravenhurst, Ontario
1930 | 90' × 12' | 1 Hall Scott | n/a | Lewis |
| MYRNO III | N. De Vaux
Lake Tahoe, CA | Luders
Stamford, CT
1922 | 50' × 10'8" | 2 6-cyl Hall-Scotts | n/a | Y 2-'22
HS |

NAME	OWNER	DESIGNER/BLDR	DIMENSIONS	ENGINE	SPEED	SOURCE
MANGASTINE	Gov. Forbes MA	Tams, Lemoine & Crane/ G. Lawley & Son Neponset, MA 1914	67′ × 8′11″ × 3′6″	2 6-cyl Speedways	n/a	R 8-'14 L. Howland
MAD WILMAR	Steve Hamilton Reno, NV	Chris Craft #5043 Algonac, MI 1929	38′ × 9′6″	1 V8 Chrysler	n/a	ACBS
MAVOURNEEN	Jim Lewis Clayton, NY	Camper & Nicholson Gosport, England 1930	50′ × 8′ × 3′6″	1 454 cu. in. V8	25 knots	Lewis

(One of six tenders built by Camper & Nicholson for the "Big Class" yacht racing of the 1920s and 1930s; British Portsmouth Reg #160944; in attendance at most ACBS shows)

NAME	OWNER	DESIGNER/BLDR	DIMENSIONS	ENGINE	SPEED	SOURCE
MARY K	John H. Kunski Detroit, MI	Hacker Boat Co. Detroit, MI 1920	40′ × 9′6″ × 3′	2 6-cyl Hall-Scotts	n/a	R 12-'20 Y 7-'22
MAROLD R #23196F	C.H. Wills Detroit, MI	The Matthews Company Port Clinton, OH 1914	100′ × 12′6″ × 3′6″	4 V12 Van Blercks, replaced by 3 Sterlings in 1926	n/a	R 9-'17 Lloyds '30
MALLARD	J.B. Chase Boston, MA	John Alden/Britt Bros. West Lynn, MA 1930	40′ × 10′ × 3′	2 6-cyl Sterlings	30 knots	R 4-'30
MARGARET FII	L.P. Fisher n/a	John Wells/Consolidated Morris Heights, NY 1925	70′ × 13′8″	2 300-hp Speedways	n/a	R 9-'25
MISS ASIA R #67912F Bing Alaba Laura	Gerry Conover Marthas Vinyard, MA	Consolidated Morris Heights, NY 1923	62′ × 12′ × 3′6″	1959: 2 V8 Palmers	n/a	Lloyds '62 CPM files

(Built for Louis Fisher of the Fisher Body Co., then owned by John Astor; laid for many years at Broward Marine, Ft. Lauderdale; brought to Essex, CT, in 1988 and beautifully restored; now at Martha's Vinyard, MA)

NAME	OWNER	DESIGNER/BLDR	DIMENSIONS	ENGINE	SPEED	SOURCE
MISS LARCHMONT IV Dormouse (IV) Nami 1940s	F. Campbell n/a W. Hadley n/a	Purdy Boat Co. Port Washington, NY 1931	40′ × 10′3″ × 2′6″ Hull #171	2 Scripps	30 knots	R 7-'25, 2- '27, 8-'31 Lloyds '31 Purdy
MISS LARCHMONT II R #45993F	Campbell Jr. n/a	Consolidated Morris Heights, NY n/a	34′ × 9′10″	1 Speedway	n/a	R 7-'25

NAME	OWNER	DESIGNER/BLDR	DIMENSIONS	ENGINE	SPEED	SOURCE
MOHICAN R #33095F	Bill Madsen n/a	Consolidated Morris Heights, NY 1929	66′ × 12′6″ × 4′	2 6-cyl Grays	n/a	Lloyds '62 CPM files

(A classic Consolidated Speedway commuter lovingly restored by the Madsens; sold to an Italian yachtsman in 1992)

NAME	OWNER	DESIGNER/BLDR	DIMENSIONS	ENGINE	SPEED	SOURCE
MYSTERY	H.P. Gibson New York, NY	Seabury/Gas Eng & Power Morris Heights, NY 1917	62′ × 9′6″ × 3′	2 6-cyl Speedways	n/a	Lloyds '25, '28
MYSTERY II	Ralph Pulitzer n/a	Tams, Lemoine & Crane/ Luders Stamford, CT 1917	71′3″ × 13′6″ × 4′5″	2 8-cyl Duesenbergs	n/a	R 9-'17, 11-'20 U.S. Combts
MONON	Morton Plant n/a	W. Hand/Robert Jacob City Island, NY 1917	55′ × 10′ × 3′	2 8-cyl Duesenbergs	35 mph	R 3-'17

(Similar to Hand's *Countess*)

NAME	OWNER	DESIGNER/BLDR	DIMENSIONS	ENGINE	SPEED	SOURCE
MEMORY Mary Ann	Henry Lippit RI RI Gov	Herreshoff Mfg. Co. Bristol, RI 1919	66′ × 11′ × 4′	2 6-cyl Sterling Dolphins	n/a	Y 1-'27
MOMO	Clinton Crane Dark Harbor, ME	Swazey/ G. Lawley & Son Neponset, MA 1915	n/a	1 Standard	n/a	MB 10-'16
MOMO II	Clinton Crane Dark Harbor, ME	Tams & King/Nevins City Island, NY 1923	40′6″ × 7′7″ × 3′	1 Speedway	n/a	Lloyds '25
MERCURY	Stavros Niarchos Athens, Greece	Peter DuCane/Vosper Southampton, England 1960	102′	3 Bristol Proteus gas turbines	n/a	Pow Yt

(Based on Brave Class of Royal Navy patrol boats; powered by three Bristol Proteus 3500-hp gas turbines for 50 knot speed; used as Mediterranean commuter)

NAME	OWNER	DESIGNER/BLDR	DIMENSIONS	ENGINE	SPEED	SOURCE
MIRAGE	Cornelius Vanderbilt n/a	Herreshoff Mfg. Co. Bristol, RI 1910	81′ × 13′	Steam	n/a	NQ #17
MARAPESSA	W.J. Matheson n/a	Mathis Camden, NJ 1916	50′ × 10′ × 2′8″	2 6-cyl Van Blercks	n/a	Van Blerck catalog

NAME	OWNER	DESIGNER/BLDR	DIMENSIONS	ENGINE	SPEED	SOURCE
NAVETTE	J.P. Morgan, Jr. E. Christopher W. Warren n/a	Herreshoff Mfg. Co. Bristol, RI 1917	114′ × 14′3″ × 3′3″	2 triple-expansion Herreshoff steam engines	n/a	Lloyds '41 CPM files

(*Navette*, meaning shuttle in French, was designed and built for Jack Morgan to be used as a smaller commuter and for the 1920 America's Cup Series. Originally powered by twin Herreshoff steam engines; Woodruff Warren installed a rotary steam engine for government testing in the early 1940s before bringing her to Florida. His two daughters lived on *Navette* as their home for more than 40 years. *Navette* is still barely afloat in southwest Florida)

NAME	OWNER	DESIGNER/BLDR	DIMENSIONS	ENGINE	SPEED	SOURCE
NANSIPAT III	V.S.M. Smith Oyster Bay, NY	Purdy & S & S/ Koch & Fyfe Glenwood Landing, NY 1937	52′3″ × 12′ × 3′	2 V12 Curtis Conquerors	n/a	Lloyds '41
NASHIRA	R.F. Hoyt Marion, MA	Consolidated Morris Heights, NY 1924	81′ × 14′6″ × 4′	2 V12 Wright Typhoons	n/a	R 2-'26, 11-'28 Y 2-'26

(First of the Consolidated houseboat-commuters; made frequent runs between Massachusetts and New York City in summers)

NAME	OWNER	DESIGNER/BLDR	DIMENSIONS	ENGINE	SPEED	SOURCE
NEREUS II Ballkim	Irving F. Marshall Boston, MA	W. McInnis/F.D. Lawley Quincy, MA 1928	75′ × 14′9″ × 3′9″	2 6-cyl Wintons	n/a	Wd Bt #52 Lloyds '31
NIAGRA IV	H. Gould n/a	n/a 1903	111′	Steam	n/a	NQ #17
NINA	Burn-Brae, Inc. W. Palm Beach, FL	Consolidated Morris Heights, NY 1925	65′ × 13′ × 4′	2 V8 Chryslers	n/a	Lloyds '74

(Also listed in Lloyds at various times as *Melba, Water Wagon, Scout, Lorna Doone*)

NAME	OWNER	DESIGNER/BLDR	DIMENSIONS	ENGINE	SPEED	SOURCE
NORTH STAR Red Wing Irene III	E. Coppage Philadelphia, PA	Consolidated Morris Heights, NY 1929	66′ × 12′6″ × 3′2″	2 Hall-Scotts 2 GM 6-71s	n/a	Lloyds '62

(A Consolidated Speedway commuter last seen at Palm Beach docks in 1987)

NAME	OWNER	DESIGNER/BLDR	DIMENSIONS	ENGINE	SPEED	SOURCE
NINA II	J. Hall Taylor Chicago, IL	Luders Marine Stamford, CT 1926	65′ × 12′ × 3′6″	2 Sterlings	29 mph	MB 11-'26 R 9-'27

NIPPER—see Saga

NAME	OWNER	DESIGNER/BLDR	DIMENSIONS	ENGINE	SPEED	SOURCE
NORTH STAR	Cornelius Vanderbilt III New York, NY	n/a 1893	256′ × 29′3″ × 16′	Steam	n/a	Vand. Book

(Used between Manhattan and Newport, RI, for almost 20 seasons)

NAME	OWNER	DESIGNER/BLDR	DIMENSIONS	ENGINE	SPEED	SOURCE
??	L. Mincus n/a	Huckins Yacht Corp. Jacksonville, FL 1929	45' × 12'	2 Kermaths	n/a	CPM files

(First commuter–Hull #C4, built by Huckins on speculation; sold at the New York boat show in 1929)

NOW THEN	Norman L. Munro New York, NY	Herreshoff Mfg. Co. Bristol, RI 1887	88' × 19'2" × 4'	1 triple-expansion steam engine	27 mph	Stm Ycht Pl Ycts Lloyds '07

(*Now Then* and *Say When* were both built for publisher and sportsman Norman Munro; *Now Then* had unsatisfactory duck-tail stern which shipped water when backing down; this was corrected with *Say When*'s normal counter)

OHEKA	Otto H. Kahn NY	Tams & King/ Henry Nevins City Island, NY 1925	61'3" × 10'7" × 3'	2 6-cyl Speedways	n/a	Lloyds '25 NQ #17
OHEKA II	Otto H. Kahn New York, NY	F. Luerssen-Maybach Vegesack, Germany 1927	73' × 12'2" × 4"	3 V12 Maybachs	42 mph	Lloyds '28 R 6-'27 Y 2-'30

(Otto Kahn, president of the Metropolitan Opera Company, Wall street financial genius, and called by Will Rogers the King of New York, brought the famed Ballets Russes and Nijinsky to America; *Oheka II* was his third commuter and was in use daily; she was of composite construction with three Maybach Zeppelin gas engines and guaranteed by the Luerssen Shipyard to do 42 mph)

OJAI	Le Roy Frost NY	Tams, Lemoine & Crane/ Julius Peterson Nyack, NY 1920	53' × 10' × 3'	n/a	n/a	R 6-'20
OJAI II	Le Roy Frost NY	Tams & King/ Julius Peterson Nyack, NY 1926	61' × 11' × 3'6"	2 6-cyl Speedways	n/a	MB 11'26
OF COURSE	J.W. Lambert n/a	Edward Fell Jardine Atlantic City, NJ 1927	42' × 10'	Scripps	35 mph	R 9-'27
OLGA	n/a	F. Luerssen Germany 1930	75' × 16' × 3'6"	2 V12 Maybachs	n/a	Y 2-'30
ONRUST	W.R. Dowling n/a	Hubert Johnson Bay Head, NJ 1939	44' × 11'6" × 3'	2 6-cyl Scripps	n/a	Y 6-'39

NAME	OWNER	DESIGNER/BLDR	DIMENSIONS	ENGINE	SPEED	SOURCE
ONYX	Herbert V. Book Detroit, MI	Great Lakes Boatbuilding Milwaukee, WI 1919	54′ × 12′ × 3′	2 6-cyl Sterlings	n/a	R 10-'25
ORCA	Malcolm Whitman New York, NY	G. Lawley & Son Neponset, MA 1922	49′ × 12′ × 2′10″	2 6-cyl Sterlings	n/a	Y 2-'22
ORIOLE	John Ettl Pt. Washington, NY	Tams Lamoine & Crane/ Peterson Nyack, NY 1919	70′4″ × 11′2″ × 4′	2 8-cyl Duesenburgs	n/a	Lloyds '25
OTTO	Mortimer Sladen Lake Windermere, England	Alfred Sladen-Forrestt Wivenhoe, England 1896	43′ × 6′ × 8′	Steam	n/a	Lk Wind

(*Otto* was a very early steam commuter on England's Lake Windermere powered by a Sessons coal-fired, triple-expansion steam engine; Alfred Sladen was a successful designer of high-speed steam launches; *Otto* is still in use and can attain 18 mph)

NAME	OWNER	DESIGNER/BLDR	DIMENSIONS	ENGINE	SPEED	SOURCE
ONEIDA	Elias C. Benedict New York, NY	John Roach Shipyard Chester, PA 1890	138′ × 20′7″ × 8′6″	Steam	n/a	CPM files

(A famous steam-yacht commuter owned by the ebullient Commodore Benedict, who cruised more than 240,000 miles in his two *Oneidas*, including daily commutes between his mansion, Indian Harbor, in Greenwich, CT, and Wall Street)

NAME	OWNER	DESIGNER/BLDR	DIMENSIONS	ENGINE	SPEED	SOURCE
ONEIDA II	Elias C. Benedict New York, NY	A.S. Cheesbrough/ Harlan & Hollingsworth Wilmington, DE 1897	201′ × 24′ × 9′	Steam	n/a	CPM files

(The second of Benedict's steam flagships, sold to William Randolph Hearst when the Commodore died in 1920)

NAME	OWNER	DESIGNER/BLDR	DIMENSIONS	ENGINE	SPEED	SOURCE
PAMNORM	N.B. Woolworth n/a	Consolidated Morris Heights, NY 1930	81′ × 13′	2 6-cyl Speedways	n/a	Y 6-'31
PAM	Bob Tiedemann Newport, RI	Great Lakes Boatbuilding Milwaukee, WI 1921	62′ × 12′ × 4′	2 Sterling Petrels	n/a	Lloyds '28 CPM files

(Owned by Hiram Walker Distillery family; used as commuter from Grosse Pointe to Detroit)

NAME	OWNER	DESIGNER/BLDR	DIMENSIONS	ENGINE	SPEED	SOURCE
PARATUS Wasp	David Gerli n/a	John Wells/ Julius Peterson Nyack, NY 1942	76′ × 18′9′ × 4′	3 Curtis Conquerors	45 mph	Lloyds 2-, 5-'42

(Originally David Gerli's commuter on Long Island Sound, later owned by Ambler family, Sarasota, FL; supposedly used in ill-fated Bay of Pigs invasion)

NAME	OWNER	DESIGNER/BLDR	DIMENSIONS	ENGINE	SPEED	SOURCE
PATTINA	Sir Charles Ross Louis Phillips New York, NY	Luders Marine Const. Stamford, CT 1917	60′ × 11′6′	2 8-cyl Duesenbergs	n/a	R 1-'17
PAULINE M R #9224F	Tom Howell Miami Beach, FL	Consolidated Morris Heights, NY 1922	57′ × 10′ × 2′10″	2 6-cyl Speedways	n/a	R 3-'23

(First of the Consolidated Speedway series of commuters)

NAME	OWNER	DESIGNER/BLDR	DIMENSIONS	ENGINE	SPEED	SOURCE
PARDON ME Lock Pat III	Jim Lewis Clayton, NY	John Hacker/Hutchinson Alexandria Bay, NY 1947	47′ × 9′4″	1 V12 Packard 4M-2500 in 1982	n/a	Lewis NQ #26

(Built for Charles P. Lyon—"King of the St. Lawrence," as he was known by the Canadian customs agents—this technically complicated and difficult-to-handle Thousand Island's comuter was sold to Dick Locke and was rarely used on Lake St. Clair. Jim Lewis bought her in the 1980s and brought her back home to the St. Lawrence. After using her for two seasons Jim gave her to the Antique Boat Museum where she can be seen today in all her chrome and mahogany glory)

NAME	OWNER	DESIGNER/BLDR	DIMENSIONS	ENGINE	SPEED	SOURCE
PERMALIA	Mark Hopkins Port Huron, MI	Herreshoff Mfg. Co. Bristol, RI 1883	100′ × 12′6″ × 5′9″	Steam	19 knots	Lou H.
PHANTOM Frolic II	F.T. Bedford Southport, CT	John Wells/ G. Lawley & Son Neponset, MA 1925	70′ × 12′6″ × 4′	2 Wintons	n/a	Lloyds '31
PHANTOM II	H. Nelson Slater NY	Consolidated Morris Heights, NY 1927	60′ × 10′7″ × 3′8′	2 6-cyl Speedways	n/a	Lloyds '31
PHANTOM R #23069F, #29113F	Ralph Pulitzer Pt. Washington, NY	Tams & King/Nevins City Island, NY 1927	66′ × 12′ × 3′ Wright Typhoons	2 V12	45 mph R 7-'27,11-'28	Lloyds '31
POLLY T	R.E. Campbell Beverly Hills, CA	Thompson Boat Co. n/a 1931	46′ × 12′ × 2′4″	2 Sterling Petrels	n/a	R 4-'31
PRETTY BETTY	Sloan Wilson NY, Miami, FL	C.D. Mower/Nevins City Island, NY 1931	54′ × 12′2″ × 3′	2 GM 4-71s	n/a	Lloyds '74 Y 7-'70

(Designed as Long Island Sound commuter by C.D. Mower [pronounced Moore] with twin Speedways;
she was owned in the 1970s by Sloan Wilson, who wrote the popular novel, *The Man in the Grey Flannel Suit*)

NAME	OWNER	DESIGNER/BLDR	DIMENSIONS	ENGINE	SPEED	SOURCE
POMANDER III	Bertram B. Conrad New Bedford, MA	W. McInnis/ G. Lawley & Son Neponset, MA 1927	85′ × 16′8′ × 4′	2 6-cyl Hall- Scotts	n/a	W Bt #52 Lloyds '31

NAME	OWNER	DESIGNER/BLDR	DIMENSIONS	ENGINE	SPEED	SOURCE
PRONTO	J. Lockerson Annapolis, MD	W. McInnis/ Chester Clement Southwest Harbor, ME 1930	55′ × 13′ × 3′	2 Chryslers	n/a	Lloyds '74

(Siimilar to *Marlin, Lindale, Bonito III*)

NAME	OWNER	DESIGNER/BLDR	DIMENSIONS	ENGINE	SPEED	SOURCE
PONJOLA	Ernest DuPont Wilmington, DE	A.S. Reed, Jr./ Marine Construction Co. Wilmington, DE 1929	39′ × 9′ × 2′8″	2 Hall-Scotts	n/a	R 2-'29 Lloyds '31
POULE D'EAU II	F. Goodwin Hartford, CT	G. Lawley & Son Neponset, MA 1930	68′ × 16′ × 4′	2 6-cyl Sterling Dolphins	n/a	Y 1-'30
PROTEST R #40214F	A.L. Lindley New York, NY	Dyer Motorcraft Co. East Greenwich, RI 1929	38′ × 10′ × 3′6″	2 Kermaths	n/a	Lloyds '31 R 8, 9-'29
PEACOCK III	Tom Eastman New York, NY	Luders Marine Const. Stamford, CT 1929	72′ × 13′6″ × 3′4″	2 6-cyl Wright Thyoons	n/a	??
PRONTO II	Ben Mozzetti Bethel Isle, CA	Stephens Brothers Stockton, CA 1928	46′ × 10′6″	2 6-cyl Sterlings	n/a	ACBS

PUZZLE—96'—A.B. Claflin (American YC)

NAME	OWNER	DESIGNER/BLDR	DIMENSIONS	ENGINE	SPEED	SOURCE
Q.E.D. R #89054F	Anthony Fokker Nyack, NY	John Atkin/Consolidated Morris Heights, NY 1938	112′ × 20′	3 total: 2 Wright Typhoons 1 Packard-Vimalert	n/a	CPM files

(Most of the advanced design and construction ideas for *Q.E.D.* came from the airplane genius of Tony Fokker, who was also a boating enthusiast—hollow masts, weldwood composite construction, advanced but practical lines. *Q.E.D.* was lent to a friend of Tony's for his wedding in 1939. This unique commuter—streamlined dark-blue hull, silver top, and white and mahogany trim—burned and sank in the Hudson in October of 1939 with the loss of one hand; fantastic short-lived craft)

NAME	OWNER	DESIGNER/BLDR	DIMENSIONS	ENGINE	SPEED	SOURCE
QUICKSILVER	C.P. Moore Osprey, FL	Huckins Yacht Corp. Jacksonville, FL 1962	53′6″ × 14′3″ × 3′10′	2 GM 6-71s	30 mph	CPM files

(Built for avid big-game fisherman who also used this Huckins Offshore model for commuting from home in Pompano Beach to Miami; purchased by author in 1979 and owned for 4 years; used on both coasts of Florida and Bahamas; a good example of what a commuter would have been in the 1950s, 1960s, and 1970s)

NAME	OWNER	DESIGNER/BLDR	DIMENSIONS	ENGINE	SPEED	SOURCE
RACCOON	Chester W. Bliss MA	W. Hand/ G. Lawley & Son Neponset, MA 1915	50′ × 10′3″ × 3′8″	2 6-cyl Van Blerks	25 mph	MB 9-'15 Y 9-'22

NAME	OWNER	DESIGNER/BLDR	DIMENSIONS	ENGINE	SPEED	SOURCE
RADIANT	Clifford Hendrix Larchmont, NY	W. Hand New Bedford, MA 1921	45′ × 10′6″ × 3′	2 6-cyl Van Blercks	n/a	Lloyds '21

(One of William Hand Jr.'s last fast powerboat designs before he turned to motorsailers)

NAME	OWNER	DESIGNER/BLDR	DIMENSIONS	ENGINE	SPEED	SOURCE
RAIDER	A.E. Walbridge New York, NY	Tams & King/ Consolidated Morris Heights, NY 1930	50′ × 12′ × 3′	2 6-cyl Speedways	n/a	Lloyds '31
RAINBOW II	Richard Joy Detroit, MI	Purdy Boat Co. Trenton, MI 1923	54′ × 12′ × 3′	2 6-cyl Speedways	n/a	Lloyds '25
RAINBOW III	R.P. Joy Detroit, MI	Consolidated Morris Heights, NY 1926	62′ × 13′ × 4′	2 Speedways	n/a	R 7-'26
RAGTIME Julie M II Little Stranger	Boothbay Boatyard Boothbay, ME	Consolidated Morris Heights, NY 1928	64′ × 12′6″ × 3′2″	2 6-cyl Speedways	n/a	Lloyds '31, '62 NQ #17

(Owned by the Hard family for years as *Little Stranger,* this Consolidated Speedway commuter passed through several more owners until she was brought to the 1989 Canadian Commuter Rendezvous by new owner Bob O'Brien of Florida. Recently bought by the Boothbay Boatyard, where much restoration work, new bottom, transom, etc., was done. Cruised from Maine to 1991 Long Island Sound Rendezvous. Now powered by Lugger diesels. Eye-catching, black-hulled beauty)

NAME	OWNER	DESIGNER/BLDR	DIMENSIONS	ENGINE	SPEED	SOURCE
RASCAL II R 34358F	Caleb Bragg Pt. Washington, NY	Purdy Boat Co. Port Washington, NY 1929	50′ × 12′ × 3′ Hull #146	2 12-cyl Packards	n/a	Lloyds '31 Y 11-'71 Purdy list

(One of the fastest commuters on Long Island Sound at 48 knots, built with step bottom for industrialist, sportsman, race car driver, raceboat driver Caleb S. Bragg; an ultra-commuter of the early thrities; a rum runner during prohibition)

NAME	OWNER	DESIGNER/BLDR	DIMENSIONS	ENGINE	SPEED	SOURCE
RAVEN I	Carl Fisher Detroit, MI	Purdy Boat Co. Indianapolis, IN 1916	50′ × 9′ × 3′3″ Hull #1	2 8-cyl Speedways	n/a	Y 11-'71 Purdy list

(The first boat built by the Purdy brothers for Carl Fisher; constructed in the infield of the Indianapolis Speedway)

NAME	OWNER	DESIGNER/BLDR	DIMENSIONS	ENGINE	SPEED	SOURCE
RAVEN II	Carl Fisher Detroit, MI	Purdy Boat Co. Indianapolis, IN 1916	46′ × 9′ × 2′	2 Speedways	n/a	Y 11-'71

(Same as above, but second boat)

NAME	OWNER	DESIGNER/BLDR	DIMENSIONS	ENGINE	SPEED	SOURCE
RAVEN III	Stewart McDonald St. Louis, MO	Purdy Boat Co. Miami Beach, FL 1917	52′ × 9′ × 2′5″	2 8-cyl Speedways	n/a	Lloyds '25

(First boat built at Purdy Boat Company's Miami Beach yard)

NAME	OWNER	DESIGNER/BLDR	DIMENSIONS	ENGINE	SPEED	SOURCE
RAVEN	H.C. Tinerman Ft. Lauderdale, FL	John Hacker/n/a Detroit, MI 1943	35′ × 9′	1 V12 Kermath	n/a	ACBS
RAVELSTON Posh Wee Joe R #83719	M. Black Toronto, Canada	John Hacker/Huskins Bay City, MI 1937	54′ × 10′	n/a	n/a	Speltz II Cls Bt 11-'87
	(Said to be on the market by anxious seller for $1 million)					
REBEL	Matthew Weissman Weston, MA	Chris Craft Series 122 Algonac, MI 1929	38′ × 9′9″ × 2′8″ Hull #5029	1 8-cyl Chrysler	n/a	CPM files
RED WING North Star	G.B. Hoppin New York, NY	Consolidated Morris Heights, NY 1929	66′ × 11′9″ × 3′4″	2 8-cyl Speedways	n/a	R 9-'29
	(One of the Consolidated Speedway series)					
REYNARD	T. Lamont New York, NY	Consolidated Morris Heights, NY 1930	75′ × 12′10″ × 3′6″	2 6-cyl Speedways	n/a	Lloyds '31 Y 5-'81 R 6-'30
RIMA	R.T. Paine II Washington, DC	G. Lawley & Son Neponset, MA 1926	68′ × 12′ × 3′8″	2 6-cyl Sterling Dolphins	n/a	R 4-'27
RED WITCH	Bob MacKay Setauket, NY	Chris Craft Series 122 Algonac, MI 1929	38′ × 9′9″ × 2′8″ Hull #5048	V8 Mercruiser 340	n/a	CPM files
RESTLESS	D.T. Wende Buffalo, NY	John Hacker/ DeFoe Shipbuilding Bay City, MI 1933	83′ × 15′ × 3′9″	2 6-cyl Sterling Dolphins	n/a	R 2-'33
ROSEWILL R #23702F	W.C. Rand Detroit, MI	John Hacker/ DeFoe Shipbuilding Bay City, MI 1926	85′ × 15′ × 3′9″	2 V12 Packards	n/a	Y 2-'27 R 3-'27
RICHELEIEU	R.S. Reynolds New York, NY	J. Wells/Consolidated Morris Heights, NY 1926	80′ × 14′6″ × 4″	2 6-cyl Wintons	n/a	Lloyds '31
ROBADORE	Robert Law Greenwich, CT	Luders Marine Const. Stamford, CT 1929	107′ × 18′10″ × 5′	2 6-cyl Wintons	n/a	Lloyds '31

NAME	OWNER	DESIGNER/BLDR	DIMENSIONS	ENGINE	SPEED	SOURCE
ROAMER III	Lee Folger	Great Lakes Boatbuilding Milwaukee, WI 1924	54′ × 11′ × 3′4″	2 6-cyl Lathrops	n/a	Lloyds '31
ROAMER II R #28269F	n/a	McInnis/ACF Wilmington, DE 1928	45′ × 11′ × 3′	2 6-cyl Hall- Scotts	n/a	Lloyds '31
RIFFIAN	R.T. Bailey New York, NY	Consolidated Morris Heights, NY 1927	54′ × 11′6″ × 3′3″	2 6-cyl Speedways	n/a	Lloyds '31
RUTH	Charles W. Selleck Atlantic High- lands, NJ	Consolidated Morris Heights, NY 1925	50′ × 11′ × 3′6″	2 6-cyl Libertys	n/a	Lloyds '25
ROCK BOTTOM	R.S. Firestone n/a	R. Hunt/Q. Adams Quincy, MA 1950	42′ × 14′5″ × 5′	1 V12 Packard	n/a	Lloyds '54
SAGA Nipper	C.P. Moore Orig: C. Payson New York, NY	John Wheeler/ Wheeler Shipyard Brooklyn, NY 1935	69′ × 13′5″ × 4′	2 V12 Packards	n/a	Lloyds '41 R 9-'35 CPM files

(Built for Charles Shipman Payson, brother-in-law of Jock Whitney. Original V12 Packards were replaced with twin V12 Wright Typhoons of 600-hp each, located well aft and driving through vee-drive gearboxes. Sold to Arthur Vining Davis to run interested prospects from Miami to Davis's Arvida land operations in the Bahama Islands. Author brought her from Davis in 1960 and used her for cruising for six years. Wright Typhoon engines were replaced with three GM 6-71 diesels)

NAME	OWNER	DESIGNER/BLDR	DIMENSIONS	ENGINE	SPEED	SOURCE
SANDS OF TIME	W. Bradford Falmouth, MA	Feadship, Inc. Holland 1956	47′11″ × 14′ × 3′3″	2 336-hp GM 8V-71s	n/a	Lloyds '62
SAGITTA	J.R. Delamer New York, NY	R.M. Haddock/NYYL&E Morris Heights, NY 1914	84′ × 40′3″ × 3′	2 200-hp 8-cyl Sterlings	n/a	R 5-'22, 5-'24 Lloyds '28
SAGA	H. Cresswell New York, NY Morris Heights, NY 1927	Sparkman & Stevens/ Consolidated	68′ × 12′ × 3′8″	2 Sterlings Coast Gd?	n/a	R 3-'27 Y 3-'27
SAGA	Charles S. Payson Pt. Washington, NY	Sparkman & Stevens/ Quincy Adams MA 1941	53′ × 12′8″ × 4′	2 6-cyl Hall- Scotts 1950: 2 GM 6-71s	n/a	Lloyds '62

NAME	OWNER	DESIGNER/BLDR	DIMENSIONS	ENGINE	SPEED	SOURCE
SANDRA II	H. Icklehs Sands Point, NY	John Wells/ Julius Peterson Nyack, NY 1942	48' × 12'3" × 2'8"	2 V12 Kermaths	n/a	MMM
SAZARAC R #12156F	George Townsend Greenwich, CT	Great Lakes Boatbuilding Milwaukee, WI 1926	54' × 11' × 3'6"	2 6-cyl Hall-Scotts	n/a	Lloyds '28
SAZARAC II R #45015F	Geroge Townsend Greenwich, CT	John Wells/Nevins City Island, NY 1930 (Caught fire and blew up in harbor in 1930s)	81' × 13'6" × 4'	2 8-cyl Wintons	n/a	R 6-'31 NQ #17 Lloyds '31
SAY WHEN	Norman Monro n/a	Herreshoff Bristol, RI 1888 (A 21-knot boat built in 1888 for Norman Munro)	138' × 14'	Herreshoff 5-cyl, quad- expansion steam	875-hp	30.5 mph
SCAMPER	N. Doubleday Garden City, NY	W. McInnis/ G. Lawley & Son Neponset, MA 1926	62' × 12'6" × 3'	2 Sterlings	35 mph	MB 9-'26 R 10-'26
SCARAMOUCHE R #12362F	H.N. Slater New York, NY	Consolidated Morris Heights, NY 1923	60' × 10'6" × 3'	2 6-cyl Speedways	30 mph	Y 7-'23 Lloyds '25
SEA BEE III	N.C. Atkinson Philadelphia, PA	Consolidated Morris Heights, NY 1938	54' × 11' × 3'3"	2 Speedways	35 mph	Lloyds '62 Y 10-'38
SEA HORSE R #6706F	James Allison James H. Snowden New York, NY	Purdy Boat Co. Trenton, MI 1921	80' × 15'6" × 4'	2 V12 Allisons	n/a	Lloyds '25
SEA PUSS II R #65759F	John T. Pratt Glen Cove, NY	Consolidated Morris Heights, NY 1946	55' × 11'6' × 3'4'	2 6-cyl Hall- Scotts	n/a	Y 3-'47 Lloyds '62
SEA PUSS R #75692F	John Pratt Glen Cove, NY	Consolidated Morris Heights, NY 1933	65' × 13' × 4'	2 V12 Wright Tornados	n/a	Lloyds '41 R 10-'33
SEA SCAMP	Charles N. Edge Milton Point, NY	G. Lawley & Son Neponset, MA 1926	42'4" × 10'2" × 2'8"	2 6-cyl Sterlings	35 mph	Y 3-'27 R 11-'34

NAME	OWNER	DESIGNER/BLDR	DIMENSIONS	ENGINE	SPEED	SOURCE
SEA HAWK Crimper	E.B. McLean Washington, DC	Consolidated Morris Heights, NY 1923	60' × 9'6" × 3'	2 6-cyl Speedways	27 mph	Lloyds '28 Y 11-'28
SHADOW III Raven I	Carl Fisher Miami Beach, FL	Purdy Boat Co. Miami Beach, FL 1916	50' × 9' Hull #1	2 6-cyl Speedways	31 mph	R 1-, 4-'17 Purdy list

(First boat built by Purdys in Indianapolis Speedway infield)

NAME	OWNER	DESIGNER/BLDR	DIMENSIONS	ENGINE	SPEED	SOURCE
SHADOW V Marionette	Carl Fisher Miami Beach, FL	Purdy Boat Co. Miami Beach, FL 1917	46' × 10'6" × 2'7" Hull #15	2 8-cyl Speedways	30 knots	R 4-'20 Y 11-'71 Purdy list

(Similar to *Altoonia, Marianne,* and *Whip* with forward cockpit; this boat set the later Purdy style of design)

NAME	OWNER	DESIGNER/BLDR	DIMENSIONS	ENGINE	SPEED	SOURCE
SHADOW FAY	Carl Fisher S.L. Slover n/a	Purdy Boat Co. Port Washington, NY 1932	60' × 14' × 3'6" Hull #186	2 V12 Allisons 2 Hall-Scotts later	n/a	R 8-'34 Y 1-, 2-'35 Purdy list
SCOUT R #Y278	August Belmont New York, NY	Herreshoff Mfg. Co. Bristol, RI 1899	81' × 10'5" × 3'	1 3-cyl Herreshoff steam engine	n/a	Steam Ycts NQ #17

(Plans and engine at Mystic Seaport Museum)

NAME	OWNER	DESIGNER/BLDR	DIMENSIONS	ENGINE	SPEED	SOURCE
SEAGULL Escape Roballis II	Edward S. Perot, Jr. Washington, DC	Consolidated Morris Heights, NY 1925	62' × 12'6" × 3'8"	2 Speedways 2 GM 6-71s (1974)	n/a	Lloyds '31 CPM files
SEASCAPE	F.T. Bedford n/a	John Wells/ Purdy Boat Co. Port Washington, NY 1942	75' × 12'9" × 3'3"	2 Hall-Scotts	n/a	CPM files

SEA OWL—mentioned in Chapter 4 of text

NAME	OWNER	DESIGNER/BLDR	DIMENSIONS	ENGINE	SPEED	SOURCE
SEABLITZ	Bradley Noyes Boston, MA	C. Raymond Hunt n/a 1949	42'	1 V12 Packard	n/a	CPM files
SHEERNESS	Marshall Sheppey Toledo, OH	Sidney Herreshoff/ Herreshoff Mfg. Co. Bristol, RI 1940	52'6" × 12' × 3"	n/a	n/a	CPM files
SHADOW VI	Carl Fisher Miami, FL	Purdy Boat Co. Miami Beach, FL 1922	43' × 10' × 2' Hull #32	2 6-cyl Speedways	n/a	R 2-'24 Purdy list

(Competed in Miami-to-Havana offshore race, put in to Key West during rough weather)

NAME	OWNER	DESIGNER/BLDR	DIMENSIONS	ENGINE	SPEED	SOURCE
SHADOW F Whisper	Carl Fisher Detroit, MI	Purdy Boat Co. Trenton, MI 1921	72′ × 14′ Hull #34	2 V12 Allisons	30+ knots	Y 11-'71 CPM files
		(Later became Herbert Pratt's Long Island commuter *Whisper*)				
SHADOW H	Carl Fisher Detroit, MI	Purdy Boat Co. Trenton, MI 1923	46′ × 10′5″ × 2′8″ Hull #54	2 6-cyl Detroit/FIAT Aero-Marine engines	31 mph	Lloyds '28 CPM files
SHADOW J	S.L. Slover Norfolk, VA	Purdy Boat Co. Trenton, MI 1924	56′ × 11′7″ × 2′8″ Hull #64	2 6-cyl Speedways 1930: 2 Hall- Scotts	n/a	Lloyds '28 CPM files
SHADOW M	Carl Fisher Detroit, MI	Purdy Boat Co. Port Washington, NY 1930	72′ × 14′2″ × 3′4″ Hull #161	2 12-cyl Allisons	n/a	Lloyds '31
SHADOW ISLE	Armand Hammer New York, NY	Consolidated Morris Heights, NY 1929	75′ × 12′10″ × 3′6″	2 GM 6-110s	n/a	Lloyds '62
SHANGRI-LA Sister II	F.L. Teeple Chicago, IL	John Hacker/Huskins Bay City, MI 1928	50′ × 13′5″ × 4′6″	2 V8 Chryslers	n/a	Lloyds '62
SKYLARK II Corisande II	Helen M. Smith New York, NY	Purdy Boat Co. Port Washington, NY 1932	65′ × 14′10″ × 4′	2 GM 6-110s	n/a	Lloyds '62
SIMOKON	Mariners' Museum Newport News, VA	Chris Craft Algonac, MI 1928	38′ × 9′9″ × 2′8″ Hull #5031	1 V8 Chris Craft	n/a	CPM files
SOCKS	F. Mina n/a	Chris Craft Algonac, MI 1928	38′ × 9′9″ × 2′8″	n/a	n/a	CPM files
SHUTTLE R #28076F	Junius S. Morgan, Jr. Glen Cove, NY	Herreshoff Mfg. Co. Bristol, RI 1928	70′ × 13′ × 3′3″	2 6-cyl Speedways	n/a	R 11-'28 Lloyds '31
SEYLON	n/a	W. McInnis/ G. Lawley & Son Neponset, MA 1928	75′ × 13′ × 4″	2 6-cyl Wintons	n/a	Y 3-'30
SKYTOP II	Robert Gould Miami, FL	Consolidated Morris Heights, NY 1949	52′ × 11′8″ × 3′6″	2 6-cyl Hall-Scotts	n/a	Lloyds '62

NAME	OWNER	DESIGNER/BLDR	DIMENSIONS	ENGINE	SPEED	SOURCE
SOX	George W. Loft n/a	Lund/Scott & Lund Erie, PA 1920	52′ × 12′ × 3′	1 V12 Liberty	n/a	Lloyds '25
SOVER- EIGN III	M.C.D. Borden New York, NY	Consolidated Morris Heights, NY 1911	166′	3 steam turbines	n/a	NQ #17 Steam Yts

(The new *Sovereign* ordered by M.C.D. Borden after his *Little Sovereign II* was beaten in an impromptu race with Peter Rouss's second *Winchester*; called "Fast Sovereign")

NAME	OWNER	DESIGNER/BLDR	DIMENSIONS	ENGINE	SPEED	SOURCE
SOURIS	William T. Grant New York, NY	W. McInnis/Nevins City Island, NY 1932	68′ × 11′10′	2 6-cyl Scripps	n/a	CPM files
SINBAD	L. Gordon Hammersley Glen Cove, NY	Tams, Lemoine & Crane/ NYYL&E Morris Heights, NY 1914	83′9″ × 14′ × 4′	2 6-cyl Twentieth Centurys	n/a	Lloyds '62
SIVA	D.F. Tripp New York, NY	Herreshoff/Britt Brothers West Lynn, MA 1928	90′ × 15′6″ × 4′6″	2 56-cyl Wintons	n/a	Lloyds '31
SPEEDALONG	William Ryle James Bennison Camden, ME	Consolidated Morris Heights, NY 1928	55′ × 11′ × 3′6″	2 Speedways	n/a	Lloyds '32, '62

(Well-kept and original Consolidated, summers on Maine coast; at Broward Marine in 1970s)

NAME	OWNER	DESIGNER/BLDR	DIMENSIONS	ENGINE	SPEED	SOURCE
SPEEDAWAY III	n/a	Ditchburn Boats Gravenhurst, Ontario Canada 1928	42′ × 9′ × 2′6″	2 6-cyl Kermaths	n/a	Lloyds '62
SPINDLE	F. Fahey Boston, MA	G. Lawley & Son Neponset, MA 1926	68′× 12′5″× 3′8″	2 Sterlings	n/a	R, Y 11-'27
STROLLER II R #33746F	C.D. Rafferty n/a	Herreshoff Mfg. Co. Bristol, RI 1930	46′ × 10′	2 6-cyl Sterling Petrels	n/a	Y 3-'30
STROLLER	1934: John Thompson Sackets Harbor, NY	Herreshoff Mfg. Co. Bristol, RI 1901	81′ × 10′7″ × 3′4″	1 3-cyl triple-expansion steam	n/a 1000 Isle	Lloyds '20

(Similar to *Scout, Clover, Jean, Lotus Seeker, Now Then*; most beautiful and quickest of the Herreshoff fast steam yachts)

NAME	OWNER	DESIGNER/BLDR	DIMENSIONS	ENGINE	SPEED	SOURCE
SPITFIRE	Reynoldson Co. n/a	Consolidated Morris Heights, NY 1930	80′ × 15′ × 4′11″	2 8-cyl GMs	n/a	Lloyds '62
SPEEJACKS	Philip K. Wrigley Chicago, IL	Consolidated Morris Heights, NY 1917	98′ × 16′ × 6′	2 Speedways	n/a	Lloyds '62 R 5-'17, 10-'25
STRANGER	George Osgood n/a	n/a 1880	180′	Steam	n/a	Salt Water Palaces
STILLETO	N.G. Herreshoff n/a	Herreshoff Mfg. Co. Bristol, RI 1885	94′ × 11′ × 4′	Steam	25 knots	LFH Steam CPM files

(Made test run on the Hudson River for 8 hours in the 1880s at 25 knots)

NAME	OWNER	DESIGNER/BLDR	DIMENSIONS	ENGINE	SPEED	SOURCE
SUSANNE	n/a	The Matthews Company Port Clinton, OH 1915	76′ × 13′6″ × 4′6″	2 300-hp Standards	n/a	CPM files
SKEDADDLE	W.R. Hearst New York, NY	J.W. Hussey/ Greenport Basin Greenport, NY 1917	60′ × 10′3″ × 4′	2 8-cyl Duesen-bergs	n/a	Lloyds '25
SUNSTAR	E.R. Foder England	Borwick Works England n/a	41′ × 9′ × 3′	2 Kermaths	n/a	R 12-'27 CPM files

(In 1927, ran regularly between the Isle of Man and the west coast of England—80 miles/day)

NAME	OWNER	DESIGNER/BLDR	DIMENSIONS	ENGINE	SPEED	SOURCE
TALLY HO	J.V. McGilvray Detroit, MI	Chris Smith/Smith Algonac, MI 1920	40′ × 9′ × 2′6″	1 V12 Liberty	n/a	Lloyds '25
TAMARACK V R #4359F	H.N. Torrey Detroit, MI	Gar Wood Algonac, MI 1927	50′ × 11′ × 3′1″	2 V12 Gar Wood Libertys	n/a	Lloyds '31 Y 2-, 12-'28
TANGO R #40430F	J.W. Hubbard New York, NY	Robinson Marine Benton Harbor, MI 1930	45′ × 11′ × 3′	2 Hall-Scotts	38 mph	Y 9-, 11-'30
TADPOLE	D.C. Shepard Neenah, WI	Alden/Britt Brothers West Lynn, MA 1933	40′ × 10′4″ × 3′	2 Sterling Petrels	n/a	R 10-'33
THANIA	n/a	Herreshoff Mfg. Co. Bristol, RI 1906	59′8′ × 10′7″ × 3′	1 Herreshoff steam engine	n/a	Herr Mus

NAME	OWNER	DESIGNER/BLDR	DIMENSIONS	ENGINE	SPEED	SOURCE
TELPERION	Ian Kennedy Toronto, Canada	Chris Craft Algonac, MI 1929	38' × 9'9" × 2'8' Hull #5020	2 283-cu in V8s	n/a	CPM files
TEMPO	Guy Lombardo NJ	John Hacker/Huskins Bay City, MI 1940	44' × 10' × 3'	n/a	n/a	CPM files

TILLIE—177' Commodore William Starbuck (American Y.C.) Steam

THYRA—76' Commodore Frank R. Lawrence (American Y.C.) Steam

NAME	OWNER	DESIGNER/BLDR	DIMENSIONS	ENGINE	SPEED	SOURCE
TEAK	A.W. Johnson Greenwich, CT	John Alden/ Luders Marine Stamford, CT 1930	n/a	1 200-hp Sterling	n/a	Y 12-'30
TEASER	Richard F. Hoyt Edsel Ford H. Osgood H. Orchard n/a	George Crouch/Nevins City Island, NY 1924	39'11" × 7'6" × 2'6"	1 V12 Wright Typhoon 1 V12 Packard Others	n/a	Lloyds '25 NQ #20 R 6-, 7-'25

(H. Osgood once refused to race with Gar Wood, saying his boat was a commuter and not a raceboat. Later if they ever got it runing right, it well could have been with 1500 hp in a 40' boat)

NAME	OWNER	DESIGNER/BLDR	DIMENSIONS	ENGINE	SPEED	SOURCE
THUNDERBIRD	George Whittell Bill Harrah Lake Tahoe, CA	John Hacker/Huskins Bay City, MI 1940	55' × 11'10' × 3'3'	2 V12 Packards 2 V12 Kermaths 2 V12 Allisons	n/a	Lloyds '41, '62, '74

(Well-known commuter; eye-catching mahogany hull with stainless-steel bridge and trunk; in use almost every day in season on Lake Tahoe)

NAME	OWNER	DESIGNER/BLDR	DIMENSIONS	ENGINE	SPEED	SOURCE
TOMAHAWK	Baddeck Trans. Co. Boston, MA	Herreshoff Mfg. Co. Bristol, RI 1920	81' × 12'7" × 3'10"	2 Speedways	n/a	Lloyds '62
T.H.C. #1	G.P. Bailey Acton, Ontario Canada	John Hacker/ Gordon Boat Co. Canada 1939	32' × 9'8" × 3'6"	2 V8 Chryslers	n/a	CPM files

(Beautifully restored; appeared at Clayton, NY, Antique Boat Show in 1991)

NAME	OWNER	DESIGNER/BLDR	DIMENSIONS	ENGINE	SPEED	SOURCE
TRADITION Dispute II	Mike & Ann Matheson Miami, FL	Chris Craft Algonac, MI 1929	38' × 9'9" × 2'8" Hull #5013	1 454 cu in V8	n/a	CPM files

(Owned by two nice old ladies on Long Island; restored by recent owners, the Mathesons, to a glittering showpiece; much-traveled, and quite good sea boat that came through with author aboard in severe summer storm on Long Island Sound during Commuters 1991)

NAME	OWNER	DESIGNER/BLDR	DIMENSIONS	ENGINE	SPEED	SOURCE
TARANTULA R #B336 & 28842	W.K. Vanderbilt New York, NY	Yarrow Torpedo Boat Ltd East London, England 1902	153'6" × 15'6" × 7'	3 Parsons steam turbines	n/a	WB #52 NQ #17

(One of the first high-speed turbine yachts, brought to U.S. by Vanderbilt and used for commuting; notorious for damage caused by her wake at high speeds)

TARANTULA II	W.K. Vanderbilt New York, NY	Clinton Crane/ G. Lawley & Son Neponset, MA 1923	n/a	2 Speedways	n/a	WB 5-'83
TUNA	J.T. Pratt New York, NY	Tams & King/ G. Lawley & Son Neponset, MA 1929	54' × 13'7" × 3'	2 6-cyl Sterlings	n/a	Y 8-'26 R 8-'26 CGD
TUNA	Mrs. J.D. Pratt New York, NY	Tams Lemoine & Crane/ G. Lawley & Son Neponset, MA 1917	70' × 10'6" × 3'3"	2 6-cyl Sterlings	n/a	Lloyds '31
TYPHOON	Edsel Ford MI	George Crouch/Nevins City Island, NY 1924	39'10" × 7'6" × 2'6"	Various	n/a	MB 1-'63

(See *Teaser*. This boat had four or five owners with four or five changes of engines—Wright Typhoon, Hall Scott, Defender, Allison, etc. Owner R.H. Hoyt commuted to the Wall Street offices of Hayden, Stone in her; Edsel Ford owned her after Hoyt. Now owned and being restored by Harold Orchard in California)

TUCK	n/a	Minnetonka Boat Works Wayzata, MN 1920	36' × 6'10"	1 6-cyl Sterling	n/a	Pr Bt 10-'30
UANI R #22062F	Curtis H. Muncie Brooklyn, NY	Luders Marine Stamford, CT 1927	42' × 9'2" × 2'6"	2 6-cyl Sterlings	n/a	R 1-'28 Lloyds '28

(Similar to *Audrey, Venus,* and four or five other production Luders commuters; used for high-speed work on Long Island Sound and Buzzards Bay in the 1930s; compact boat with striking lines)

ULTIMA DEA	Gianni Agnelli Turin, Italy	Renato Levi/Baglietto Varazze, Italy 1962	36' × 12'6" × 2'	3 V8 Maseratis	50+ mph	R Levi p 31

(One of Renato Levi's first deep-vee offshore-competition cabin boats; with three Maserati 4.9 litre V8s ran at 50 mph; excellent rough-water express cruiser used by Fiat chief Gianni Agnelli for offshore racing and later for commuting on the Mediterranean)

NAME	OWNER	DESIGNER/BLDR	DIMENSIONS	ENGINE	SPEED	SOURCE
UNIQUE	C.B. Lockwood Sandusky, OH	C.C. Smith Boat & Engine Co Algonac, MI 1920	35' × 9'5" × 2'10"	1 V12 Smith-built Liberty	n/a	Lloyds '25
UTOPIA	E.A. Onthank Boston, MA	A.E. Luders/ Luders Marine Stamford, CT 1915	50' × 10'3" × 3'	1 6-cyl Van Blerck	n/a	Lloyds '25
VAN I	Curtis H. Muncie Brooklyn, NY	Luders Marine Stamford, CT 1927	42' × 9'2" × 2'6"	1 6-cyl Sterling	n/a	R 11-'28
VALJORA Delight	J. Snigorski Boston, MA R. Tollenger Boston, MA (Being restored in Boston)	F.W. Lawley/ G. Lawley & Son Neponset, MA 1918	62' × 12' × 4'	2 8-cyl Speedways	n/a	Lloyds '62
VAMOOSE R #Y-323 R #Y27488	W.R. Hearst San Francisco, CA	Hereshoff Mfg. Co. Bristol, RI 1890—01	112'5" × 12'4" × 7'	1 quadruple- expansion steam engines	n/a	Stm Yt Intro Ycht

(Similar to *Say When, Ballymena, Now Then*, the early Herreshoff express commuter-cruisers. *Vamoose* was a little faster with the Herreshoff, five-cylinder, quadruple-expansion engine. About 23-24 knots was achieved. Used successfully by many owners until the 1920s. Speaks well for Herreshoff's strong, light construction)

NAME	OWNER	DESIGNER/BLDR	DIMENSIONS	ENGINE	SPEED	SOURCE
VAMOOSE	Charles Lyon Oak Island, NY	Fitzgerald & Lee Alexandria Bay, NY 1930	38' × 9'9" × 3'	Scripps	n/a	Y 10-'36 Speltz
VAMOOSE II	Charles Lyon Oak Island, NY	John Hacker/ Fitzgerald & Lee Alexandria Bay, NY 1938	45' × 10' × 3'	2 6-cyl Hall- Scotts	40+ mph	R 10-'36 MBt 10-'36 Y 10-'36
VAMOOSE	Richard F. Hoyt New York, NY	Consolidated Morris Heights, NY 1914	61' × 10'9" × 3'	2 V12 Wright Typhoons	n/a	Lloyds '31

(Richard Hoyt also owned noted commuters *Nashira* and *Teaser*)

NAME	OWNER	DESIGNER/BLDR	DIMENSIONS	ENGINE	SPEED	SOURCE
VANSANTA R #28548F	George Pynchon New York, NY	Consolidated Morris Heights, NY 1928	92' × 16' × 4'	2 6-cyl Speedways	n/a	R 11-'28 Lloyds '28
VEDETTE	M.C.D. Borden Atlantic Highlands, NJ	Herreshoff Mfg. Co. Bristol, RI 1890	124'	Steam	n/a	NQ #17

NAME	OWNER	DESIGNER/BLDR	DIMENSIONS	ENGINE	SPEED	SOURCE
VENUS R #35159F	J.K. Reckford New York, NY	Luders Marine Stamford, CT 1929	42' × 8'6" × 3'6"	1 6-cyl Sterling	n/a	Y 10-'30 Lloyds '31
VENUS III	J.K. Reckford New York, NY	Luders Marine Stamford, CT 1930	50' × 11'3" × 3'6"	2 6-cyl Sterlings	n/a	Lloyds'31
VAMPIRE Phantom	C.F. Lincoln Ralph Pulitzer New York, NY	Tams & King/Nevins City Island, NY 1927	66' × 12' × 3'	2 V12 Wright Typhoons	n/a	Plans #H604 Lloyds '31
VAGABOND	Henry S. Lewis n/a	Consolidated Morris Heights, NY 1930	45' × 9'10" × 3"	2 Kermaths	n/a	Jim Lewis
VARRAMISTA Sinbad	James Ottley Glen Cove, NY	Cox & Stevens/ Consolidated Morris Heights, NY 1926	68' × 12' × 3'	2 6-cyl Speedways	n/a	Lloyds '31
VIA WATER	Paul Strasburg Detroit, MI	John Hacker/ Hacker Boat Co. Detroit, MI 1923	50' × 10' × 3'	2 V12 Libertys	n/a	Lloyds '25
VITESSE	Gen. Brayton Ives Ossining, NY	Consolidated (C. Seabury) (C. Seabury) Morris Heights, NY 1905–6	140'	2 2-cyl Seaburys steam engines	n/a	Stm Ychts NQ #17
VIVACE	n/a	Consolidated Morris Heights, NY 1911	86'	Steam	n/a	Y 2-'36
VIXEN	Adolph M. Dick New York, NY	Consolidated Morris Heights, NY 1929	76' × 14' × 3'6"	2 6-cyl Speedways	n/a	Lloyds'31 R 12-'29
VERDI	Walter Green Utica, NY	Will Gardner/ Consolidated Morris Heights, NY 1909	75' × 11'5" × 4'	2 6-cyl Speedways	n/a	Lloyds'13, '20
VENETIAN MAID	L.W. Tuller Detroit, MI	C. Wilby/American Boat n/a 1916	60' × 10' × 3'	2 8-cyl Van Blercks	n/a	Van Blerck catalog

NAME	OWNER	DESIGNER/BLDR	DIMENSIONS	ENGINE	SPEED	SOURCE
VEGA II	n/a	F. Lurssen Germany 1928	77′ × 13′ × 4′	2 Maybachs	n/a	Levick Col Ycht
VOLKERTSE II	Paul Veeder New York, NY	Purdy Boat Co. Port Washington, NY 1932	65′ × 14′ × 4′ Hull #177	2 6-cyl Speedways	n/a	R 5-, 9-'32
VOLKERTSE	Paul Veeder Hewlett, NY	William Atkin/ Chute & Bixby Huntington, NY 1930	57′8″ × 12′6″ × 3′	2 6-cyl Sterlings	n/a	Lloyds '31
VITESSE	J. Vietor New York, NY	Consolidated Morris Heights, NY 1932	82′ × 14′6″ × 4′	2 V12 Wright Typhoons	n/a	R 12-'27

(Consolidated houseboat design similar to *Ardea, Kegonsa, Iota, Lone Star, Nashira*, and *Zinganee*, all fast with twin V12 Wright Typhoons)

NAME	OWNER	DESIGNER/BLDR	DIMENSIONS	ENGINE	SPEED	SOURCE
VORTEX	Harold Vanderbilt New York, NY	Purdy/Herreshoff Mfg. Co. Bristol, RI 1928	150′ × 25′ × 8′	2 V12 Triebers	n/a	Lloyds '28

VANISH—another early (1880s?) Herreshoff steam flyer

VETO—115′ American Y.C. commuter—1890s—George Law

NAME	OWNER	DESIGNER/BLDR	DIMENSIONS	ENGINE	SPEED	SOURCE
WARRIOR	Charles Shipman Payson New York, NY	Cox & Stevens/ Julius Peterson Nyack, NY 1925	38′ × 11′6″ × 3′	2 6-cyl Hall-Scotts	n/a	Lloyds '31
WASP	Cameron B. Waterman Grosse Pointe, MI	Great Lakes Boatbuilding Milwaukee, WI 1923	65′ × 12′ × 4′	2 6-cyl Sterlings	n/a	Lloyds '28
WASP	Everett P. Read New Bedford, MA	John Hacker/Robinson Benton Harbor, MI 1929	39′ × 8′6″ × 2′6″	1 6-cyl Hall-Scott	n/a	Lloyds '31
WASP	Philip K. Wrigley Catalina Island, CA	Henry C. Grebe/ Great Lakes Boatbuilding Chicago, IL 1931	46′ × 10′10″ × 3′	2 6-cyl Sterlings	n/a	Lloyds '31

NAME	OWNER	DESIGNER/BLDR	DIMENSIONS	ENGINE	SPEED	SOURCE
WASP	Philip K. Wrigley Chicago, IL	Henry C. Grebe/ Great Lakes Boatbuilding Chicago, IL 1931	94' × 16'2" × 4'6"	2 8-cyl Sterling Vikings II	n/a	Lloyds '41
WASP	D. Geril n/a	Wells/Peterson Nyack, NY 1942	76'4" × 18'7" × 4'	3 Viz Curtises	n/a	Lloyds '67
WAYFARER	Richard K. LaBlond Cincinnati, OH	John Wells/Matthews Port Clinton, OH 1914	59'10" × 12' × 3'	2 6-cyl Speedways	n/a	Lloyds '31
WAYFARER	Frank McQuesten Boston, MA	G. Lawley & Son Neponset, MA 1926	68' × 12'5" × 3'8"	2 6-cyl Sterlings	n/a	Lloyds '31
WAYFARER Cyric	Winthrop W. Aldrich New York, NY	Henry Gielow/ G. Lawley & Son Neponset, MA 1929	104' × 17' × 4'6"	2 6-cyl Wintons	n/a	Lloyds'31
WAYFARER	Jeff Domzalski Roseville, MI	Monmouth Marine Keyport, NJ 1938	40' × 11'	2 V8 Crusaders	n/a	CPM files
WELCOME	W.E. John Rye, NY	G. Lawley & Son Neponset, MA 1910	72' × 14' × 4'9"	2 GM 6-71s	n/a	Lloyds '62
WIGWAG	H.S. Borden New York, NY	Consolidated Morris Heights, NY 1924	62' × 10'6" × 3'	2 6-cyl Speedways	n/a	Lloyds '25 R 11-'25
WINARA	Edward B. Henry Detroit, MI	E. Lockwood Haggas/ NYYL&E Morris Heights, NY 1927	47' × 10'6" × 2'	2 6-cyl Capitol Libertys	n/a	CPM files
W.J. CONNERS III	W.J. Conners Buffalo, NY	Gar Wood Algonac, MI 1922	50' × 10'3" × 3'	2 V12 Libertys	n/a	Lloyds '25
WESTERLY	E.W. Murphy Los Angeles, CA	W. McInnis/Edgar Ames Seattle, WA 1920	64' × 12'3" × 4'	2 V12 Capitol Libertys	n/a	Lloyds '28

NAME	OWNER	DESIGNER/BLDR	DIMENSIONS	ENGINE	SPEED	SOURCE
WINDERMERE	Louis P. Bach Greenwich, CT	Fred Lord/ Ruddock Boat Co. Greenwich, CT 1926	45′ × 10′ × 2′6″	1 8-cyl Fiat	n/a	R 2-'27
WIND ROSE	James Nelson Larry M. Weinzetl n/a	A.C.F. Wilmington, DE 1928	54′ × 12′ × 3′	2 6-cyl Hall- Scotts	n/a	Lloyds '31

(Originally built as *Sea King* for a gentleman whose name really was Sailing W. Baruch; was used on the Great Lakes as a submarine patrol craft; none were sighted. Now being restored by enthusiastic and capable group in Minneapolis)

NAME	OWNER	DESIGNER/BLDR	DIMENSIONS	ENGINE	SPEED	SOURCE
WHEW	E. Sohier Welch Boston, MA	F. Lawley/ G. Lawley & Son South Boston, MA 1905	35′8″ × 7′6″ × 3′	1 6-cyl Sterling	n/a	Lloyds '25
WHIM Gar Jr.	Albert L. Smith Philadelphia, PA	Gar Wood Algonac, MI 1923	50′ × 10′3″ × 3′	2 V12 Libertys	n/a	Lloyds '29
WHIM III Wahoo R #29995F	Harrison Williams New York, NY	Tams & King/ Consolidated Morris Heights, NY 1928	56′ × 12′ × 3′6″	2 V12 Wright Typhoons	n/a	Lloyds '28, '41 R 11-'28

(Another of Harrison Williams' fast commuters—52 mph with original step bottom; looked like a government patrol craft; last seen in Victoria, British Columbia, in the 1960s)

NAME	OWNER	DESIGNER/BLDR	DIMENSIONS	ENGINE	SPEED	SOURCE
WHIRLWIND Yado	Julius Fleishmann Port Washington, NY	Consolidated Morris Heights, NY 1922	62′ × 10′6″ × 3′3″	2 6-cyl Speedways	n/a	Lloyds '25 MB 6-'26

(*Whirlwind* won the Express Cruiser Race in Miami in the winter of 1923)

NAME	OWNER	DESIGNER/BLDR	DIMENSIONS	ENGINE	SPEED	SOURCE
WHISPER R #9963	Herbert L. Pratt Roslyn, NY	Purdy Boat Co. Trenton, MI 1921	72′ × 14′4″ × 3′	2 V12 Allisons	n/a	Lloyds '25, '28 NQ #17

(A beautiful example of Purdy Brothers design and craftsmanship; known as *Shadow F* when owned by Carl Fisher)

NAME	OWNER	DESIGNER/BLDR	DIMENSIONS	ENGINE	SPEED	SOURCE
WHIPPET	Oliver Jennings n/a	W.J. Hussey/ Greenport Basin Greenport, NY 1916	60+′ × 12′ × 4′	2 6-cyl Van Blercks	n/a	MB 9-'17 Van Blerck catalog
WINCHESTER Adroit	Peter Rouss New York, NY	H.J. Gielow/Robert Jacob City Island, NY 1907	141′5″ × 15′5″ × 5′	2 reciprocating steam engines	n/a	Stm Yt R 2-'22

(The first of the four fast, no-nonsense commuters built for Peter Winchester Rouss, ambitious son of Charles Broadway Rouss, and used for commuting to Manhattan from Oyster Bay)

NAME	OWNER	DESIGNER/BLDR	DIMENSIONS	ENGINE	SPEED	SOURCE
WINCHESTER II Flying Fox	Peter Rouss New York, NY	Cox & King/Yarrow Glasgow, Scotland 1909	165' × 15'6" × 5'	3 Parsons steam turbines	n/a	Stm Ycht R 10-'17

(A second and more aggressive *Winchester*; after Peter Rouss, she was sold to four experienced yachtsmen in succession, then sold to the Colombian Navy whereupon she served another 17 years after already having been a commuter for 40 years)

NAME	OWNER	DESIGNER/BLDR	DIMENSIONS	ENGINE	SPEED	SOURCE
WINCHESTER III Trillora	Peter Rouss New York, NY	Cox & Stevens/Yarrow Glasgow, Scotland 1912	205' × 18'6" × 6'	2 Yarrow steam turbines	n/a	Stm Ycht R 2-'22

(Peter was really pushing commuter limits with this one; she was nevertheless a vessel coveted by many smaller navies)

NAME	OWNER	DESIGNER/BLDR	DIMENSIONS	ENGINE	SPEED	SOURCE
WINCHESTER IV enard R #76998F	Peter Rouss New York, NY	Cox & Stevens/ Bath Iron Works Bath, ME 1915	225' × 21' × 7'	2 Bath-built steam turbines	n/a	Stm Ycht R 2-'22

(Designed by Bruno Tornroth and built in the U.S., she was a study in good-natured ostentation—much more of a statement than today's mega-yachts. Peter Winchester's favorite *Winchester*, she was used in both World War I and II, and owned at various times by intrepid yachtsmen of the Astor and Vanderbilt clans—the third Cornelius Vanderbilt died aboard in 1942)

NAME	OWNER	DESIGNER/BLDR	DIMENSIONS	ENGINE	SPEED	SOURCE
WIGWAM Toots III	David Wallace Detroit, MI	John Hacker/Huskins Bay City, MI 1930	45' × 11' × 3'	2 V8 Chryslers	n/a	Lloyds '41
WILD GOOSE II	H.T. Bent Hampton, VA	L.C. McInnis/A.C.F. Wilmington, DE 1929	40'3" × 11'4" × 3'	1 6-cyl Hall Scott	n/a	Lloyds '41
WILD GOOSE III	James M. West Beaufort, NC	acf Wilmington, DE 1930	54'8" × 12' × 3'10"	2 6-cyl Hall-Scotts	n/a	Lloyds '41
WILD KNIGHT	Francis F. Chase Boston, MA	B.T. Dobson/ William Wood New Bedford, MA 1932	60' × 12' × 4'	2 V12 Libertys	n/a	Lloyds '41
WINDWARD	Matthew J. Hall Great Neck, NY	Chris Craft Algonac, MI 1929	38' × 9'9" × 3'	1 V8 Chris Craft	n/a	Lloyds '41
WINGS	Alex Verity Freeport, NY	Chris Craft Algonac, MI 1929	38' × 9'9" × 3'	1 V8 Chris Craft	n/a	Lloyds '41

NAME	OWNER	DESIGNER/BLDR	DIMENSIONS	ENGINE	SPEED	SOURCE
WHIP	Robert Maypole n/a	Purdy Boat Co. Miami Beach, FL 1919	42' × 9'2" × 2'3" Hull #21	2 6-cyl Speedway	30 mph	CPM files
WONDERFUL ONE	H.C. Stutz n/a	Consolidated Morris Heights, NY 1925	64' × 14' × 3'6"	2 6-cyl Speedways	n/a	Lloyds '25
YANK S.P908	George R. Dyer New York, NY	Tams, Lemoine & Crane/ Julius Peterson Nyack, NY 1917	60' × 10'5" × 6'	2 6-cyl Speedways	n/a	Lloyds '25
YOU'LL DO	Walter E. Sachs Bridgeport, CT	A.E. Luders/ Luders Marine Stamford, CT1922 1922	49'11" × 10'6" × 3'	1 6-cyl Sterling Petrel	n/a	Lloyds '25
YANKEE	Sherman Fairchild Oyster Bay, NY	F.K. Lord/ G. Lawley & Son Neponset, MA 1929	56' × 12'3" × 3'	2 V12 Libertys	40 mph	Lloyds '31
YAWDRO	Fred A. Ordway Boston, MA	John Wells/ G. Lawley & Son Neponset, MA 1926	65' × 12'2" × 3'	2 6-cyl Sterlings	n/a	Lloyds '28
YOU'LL DO II	W.E. Sachs Darien, CT	A.E. Luders/ Luders Marine Stamford, CT 1922	72' × 13'6" × 3'	2 8-cyl Sterlings	n/a	Lloyds '31
YO HO HO II	Caleb S. Bragg New York, NY	Purdy Boat Co./ Consolidated Morris Heights, NY 1929	50' × 11' × 3'6"	2 6-cyl Speedways	n/a	Lloyds '31

Another successful Purdy design, this one being built by Consolidated for sportsman Bragg; not as fast or as striking as his other Purdy commuter *Rascal*. Caleb Bragg owned these two Purdys and the 82' *Masquerader* all at the same time.)

NAME	OWNER	DESIGNER/BLDR	DIMENSIONS	ENGINE	SPEED	SOURCE
ZIPPER II Altonia	Mike Matheson Miami, FL	Ned Purdy/Purdy Boat Co. Miami Beach, FL 1919	42' × 9' × 2'3"	2 6-cyl Speedways	n/a	Lloyds '28

(Built originally for Carl Fisher, later owned by John Stroh of the brewing family, and currently part of the Matheson collection; now powered by twin Sterlings)

NAME	OWNER	DESIGNER/BLDR	DIMENSIONS	ENGINE	SPEED	SOURCE
ZIPPER	Antique Boat Museum Clayton, NY	Purdy Brothers/ Les Staudacher Bay City, MI 1975	43′ × 9′10″ × 3′	2 V8	n/a	WB #80

(John Stroh had this boat built by Les Staudacher of raceboat-building fame. Stroh had an early set of Purdy plans for a Stroh-family commuter that was never built and this *Zipper* was constructed to those plans in 1975. She is currently owned and is in commission at the Antique Boat Museum in Clayton, NY)

NAME	OWNER	DESIGNER/BLDR	DIMENSIONS	ENGINE	SPEED	SOURCE
ZULA	Elmer A. Sperry Bellport, NY	F.K. Lord/ Ruddock Boat Co. NY 1925	33′6″ × 8′6″ × 2′6″	1 6-cyl Scripps	n/a	Lloyds '28
ZALOPHUS, JR Major	John Ringling New York, NY, Sarasota, FL	Consolidated Morris Heights, NY 1920	55′ × 10′6″ × 3′	2 6-cyl Speedways	n/a	Lloyds '25, '31
ZAMETTE	Z.G. Simmons, Jr. Greenwich, CT	A.C.F. Wilmington, DE 1927	47′ × 10′6″ × 3′6″	1 6-cyl Hall Scott	n/a	Lloyds '28
ZINGANEE II	Edward S. Moore New York, NY	Consolidated Morris Heights, NY 1926	81′ × 14′6″ × 4′	2 V12 Wright Typhoons	28 mph	Lloyds '28

(One of the half-dozen or so of the fast Consolidated houseboat-commuters. Not much on looks, they were quick and comfortable. None survive)

NAME	OWNER	DESIGNER/BLDR	DIMENSIONS	ENGINE	SPEED	SOURCE
ZINGANEE	Morgan Barney New York, NY	N.G. Herreshoff/ Herreshoff Mfg. Co. Bristol, RI 1902	81′ × 10′7′ × 3′	1 Herreshoff steam engine	n/a	Lloyds '25
ZIPALONG Gansetta	A.H. Henderson New York, NY	Swasey, Raymond & Page/G. Lawley & Son South Boston, MA 1907	79′ × 11′ × 3′6″	1 6-cyl Standard	n/a	Lloyds '28
ZIPALONG	E.W. Clark Philadelphia, PA	Consolidated Morris Heights, NY 1927	50′ × 10′ × 3′2″	1 6-cyl Speedway	n/a	Lloyds '28
ZANTRE	Booth Tarkington n/a	Clement Clark Kennebunk, ME 1931	40′	2 6-cyl Kermaths	n/a	R 12-'31
ZIG ZAG	Conrad Stein New York, NY	A.E. Luders/ Luders Marine Stamford, CT 1916	44′ × 7′6″ × 3	1 8-cyl Van Blerck	n/a	Van Blerck catalog

Bibliography

―――――――

PERIODICALS

Lloyd's Register of American Yachts. New York: Lloyd's Register of Shipping, 1903–1976.

Motorboat (The Pioneer—The Authority). New York: Motorboat.

Motor Boating & Sailing. New York: Hearst.

Nautical Quarterly. Vols. 1–50. New York: Nautical Quarterly.

The Rudder. America's First Boating Magazine. New York: Rudder.

WoodenBoat. Brooklin, Maine: WoodenBoat.

Yachting. New York: Yachting Publishing.

Angelucci, Enzo, and Peter Bowers. *The American Fighter.* New York: Orion, Crown, 1987.

Atkin, William. *Of Yachts and Men.* New York: Sheridan House, 1949.

Barrett, James Lee. *Steamboat Kings.* : Michigan Heritage Library, 1986.

Berton, Elliot, and P. R. Ward. *Motor Craft Encyclopedia.* : Barse & Hopkins, 1912.

Bonsall, Thomas E. *The Lincoln Motorcar.* Baltimore: Bookman, 1981.

Carse, Robert. *Rum Row.* New York: Rinehart, 1959.

Carter, Samuel. *The Boatbuilders of Bristol.* New York: Doubleday, 1970.

Crane, Clinton H. *Yachting Memories.* New York: Van Nostrand, 1952.

Desmond, Kevin. *Power Boats.* London: Conway Maritime Press, 1988.

Dockey, Philip S. *The Liberty Engine.* Washington, D.C.: Smithsonian Institute Press, 1968.

Farmer, Weston. *From My Old Boat Shop.* Camden, Maine: International Marine Publishing, 1979.

Fox, Uffa. *Seamanlike Sense in Powercraft.* : Peter Davis, 1968.

Fox, Uffa. *Uffa Fox's Second Book.* New York: Scribner's, 1935.

Friedman, Norman. *U.S. Small Combatants.* Annapolis: Naval Institute Press, 1987.

Hendry, Maurice. "Col. Jessie G. Vincent," *Special Interest Autos,* June 1978.

Herreshoff, L. Francis. *Capt. Nat Herreshoff: Wizard of Bristol.* New York: Sheridan House, 1953.

Hofman, Erik. *The Steam Yachts.* Tuckahoe, N.Y.: John de Graff, 1970.

Johnson, Robert Erwin. *Guardians of the Sea.* Annapolis: Naval Institute Press, 1987.

Josephson, Matthew. *The Robber Barons.* New York: Harcourt Brace, 1962.

Kimes, Beverly Rae. *Packard: A History.* Princeton, N.J.: Automobile Quarterly Publications, 1978.

King, H. F. *Aero-Marine Origins.* New York: Putnam, 1966.

Klingman, William. *1919.* New York: St. Martin's, 1987.

Levi, Renato Sunny, *Dhows to Deltas.* Hampshire, England: Nautical, 1971.

Lord, Lindsay. *Naval Architecture of Planing Hulls.* Cambridge, Md.: Cornell Maritime Press, 1963.

Matz, Mary. *The Many Lives of Otto Kahn.* New York: Macmillan, 1963.

Mercier, Gilbart B. *Pleasure Yachts of the Thousand Islands.* Clayton, N.Y.: Shipyard Museum Press, 1981.

Moore, Winthrop P. *Motorboats.* New York: Dodd, Mead, 1946.

Mudie, Colin, and Rosemary Mudie. *Power Yachts.* London: Granada, 1977.

Page, Victor W. *Modern Aviation Engines.* New York: Henley, 1929.

Parker, Marion, and Robert Tyrrell. *Rumrunner.* Seattle: Orca, 1988.

Parkinson, John, Jr. *The History of the New York Yacht Club.* 2 vols. New York: NYYC, 1975.

Pattinson, George H. *The Great Age of Steam on Lake Windermere.* Kendal, England: Titus Wilson & Son, 1981.

Phillips-Birt, D. *Famous Speedboats of the World.* City?, England: Muller Publishing, 1956.

Preston, Antony. *Strikecraft.* London: Bison, 1982.

Seabury, Charles L. *Steam Launches and Marine Equipment.* Morris Heights, N.Y.: , 1901.

Sinclair, Andrew. *Prohibition: The Era of Excess.* New York: Little, Brown, 1962.

Sloat, Warren. *1929—America before the Crash.* New York: Macmillan, 1979.

Speltz, Bob. *The Real Runabouts.* Vols 1–3, 5. Lake Mills, Iowa: Graphic. 1977–88.

Stephens, William P. *Traditions and Memories of American Yachting.* Brooklin, Maine: WoodenBoat, 1989.

Strickland, Frederic. *Motor Boats.* New York: Pitman, 1923.

Taylor, C. Fayette. *Aircraft Propulsion.* Washington, D.C.: Smithsonian Institution Press, 1971.

Thornycroft, John I. *Short History of Small Torpedo Boats.* Cheswick, England: Thornycroft, 1919.

Thruelsen, Richard. "The Fabulous Jock Whitney," *Saturday Evening Post,* May–June, 1957.

Willoughby, Malcolm F. *Rum War at Sea.* Washington, D.C.: Government Printing Office, 1964.

Index